# Surviving Minnesota WINTER

## A Guide for Newcomers & Residents Alike

by Brett Ortler

Adventure Publications, Inc.
Cambridge, MN

## Dedication

To my wife and children for their love and support in all that I do.

Thanks to Isanti Mayor George Wimmer for his clarification regarding city vs. county snow plowing policy and to Dale Ortler and Andy Cummings for information regarding the Canadian Pacific Christmas Train. Also, many thanks to Judith Kissner of Scout & Morgan Books (www.scoutandmorganbooks.com) for reviewing the book, and to Ryan Jacobson for reviewing the book as well, and for his copyediting expertise.

Cover and book design by Lora Westberg and Jonathan Norberg

10 9 8 7 6 5 4 3 2 1

Copyright 2015 by Brett Ortler
Published by Adventure Publications, Inc.
820 Cleveland Street South
Cambridge, MN 55008
1-800-678-7006
www.adventurepublications.net
All rights reserved
Printed in U.S.A.

ISBN: 978-1-59193-589-6

# Table of Contents

# Table of Contents

# Table of Contents

# Introduction

So you're living in Minnesota for the winter! Well, whether you're a long-suffering resident or a recent transplant, there's no way around it: you're going to be cold, at least some of the time. But that doesn't mean you have to be miserable. On the contrary, with a little preparation, it's not hard to stay warm, find something new that's fun to do and even learn to enjoy (at least some) aspects of the weather, such as sun dogs and other wintertime meteorological phenomena.

Born and raised in Minnesota, I'm going to cover everything from the basics that new transplants need to know to fun facts and little-known aspects of winter. Above all, I'll try my best to be entertaining as I know all too well how humorless it is to grudgingly shovel out from an Easter weekend snowstorm or to dig out from a foot and a half of snow when just a few inches were forecasted.

So bust out your boots, throw on a bomber hat and a warm coat, and let's get outdoors and start enjoying winter!

# What to Expect, Month by Month
## (monthly averages in the Twin Cities)

## September   HIGH: 72° ✻ LOW: 52° ✻ AVERAGE SNOWFALL: trace

Even though September marks the beginning of fall and can offer some of the finest weather around, it also serves as a reminder of fall's inevitable slide toward winter, or at least weather that feels like winter for those who have spent the summer lounging by the lakes. September's weather can vary significantly. One week might be 80 and sunny but the week after the temps are in the 50s or (gasp) the 40s.

**What to Expect:** When it comes to real winter weather, you don't really have to worry much in September. Sure, the weather may turn colder, but just use that as an excuse to buy sweaters.

## October   HIGH: 58° ✻ LOW: 40° ✻ AVERAGE SNOWFALL: 0.6" (8.1" in 1991)

The metro area usually sees its first measurable snowfall in October. What's a measurable snowfall, you ask? A tenth of an inch or more. And if it's going to snow, the temperature has to drop, and October is when the mercury really starts to fall.

**What to Expect:** Just because a snowfall is measurable doesn't mean you have to worry about shoveling; these early snowfalls are usually just dustings and don't last. Still, it's always a good idea to have your shovels/snowblower/winter gear ready by late October. That's because Jack Frost sometimes visits in October. I tramped through the Halloween Blizzard of 1991, which dropped 28.4 inches of snow from October 31 to November 3. (Even though two of my Halloween costumes literally disintegrated, I soldiered on, filling an entire pillowcase with candy.)

## November

HIGH: 41° ✳ LOW: 26° ✳ AVERAGE SNOWFALL: 9.3" (46.9" in 1991)

If you're wondering when you can expect the first inch of snow, the betting money is on November. The average date of our first inch of snow occurs around November 18, and the average daily high in November drops almost 20 degrees. Snowfall can quickly begin to pile up; in fact, the snowiest month on record in the Twin Cities isn't a January or a February, it's November of 1991 (thanks in large part to the 1991 Halloween Blizzard). Even when it's not snowy, it can be a bit drab. On average, more than half the days are cloudy, second only to December.

**What to Expect:** It's time to bust out the shovels and hats with earflaps. While November isn't usually particularly cold in the Twin Cities area—the average maximum daily temperatures at the beginning of the month are still usually in the 40s—the bottom begins to drop out as the month proceeds. By the end of the month, the max temperatures are only in the 30s, and snow begins to stick around. Then again, on occasion, November storms can wallop the state with heavy snow (paging 1991!), and it can also turn quite cold. Record November lows have dipped well below zero. If you don't have suitable winter gear and snow removal equipment, get some post-haste. If you wait until the first storm, you'll likely find the shelves pretty spare.

## December

HIGH: 27° ✳ LOW: 12° ✳ AVERAGE SNOWFALL: 11.9" (33.6" in 2010)

Like November, December is cloudy—and increasingly cold. With average maximum temps just at or below freezing, ice begins shrouding the lakes. By the time Christmas rolls around, the average highs are in the low 20s, with average lows in the upper single digits. The winter solstice—the shortest day of the year—occurs in December; only about 8 hours and 46 minutes separate sunrise from sunset. (By contrast, the summer solstice is over 15 hours and 37 minutes; that's almost an entire workday's worth of extra light!)

**What to Expect:** You'll obviously need to dress warmly, but December often marks the beginning of winter fun! December sees a fair amount of snow, and there is often at least some snow on the ground. If you're lucky, it's enough for fun activities like snowmobiling or snowshoeing. Better yet, the first winter snows are often some of the prettiest because the landscape is essentially unblemished (not to mention that the cities are mostly free of road salt residue and traffic sludge). So if you see some big flakes coming down, consider tramping around outside with a camera and catching some wintertime shots. And if you can brave the cold, take advantage of the short days by doing some stargazing on a clear night. Some of the best constellations can be seen in the winter (Orion among them), and the short days make it easy to stargaze without having to stay up late.

Depending on where you live, you may begin to see folks ice fishing on the lakes. Of course, before you venture out onto the lakes in pursuit of a new walleye record, always be sure the ice is thick enough/solid enough. For more on ice safety, see page 123.

## January   HIGH: 23° ✳ LOW: 7° ✳ AVERAGE SNOWFALL: 12.2" (46.4" in 1982)

January is a strange month. In the Twin Cities, it's the coldest month of the year, on average, and in terms of total average snowfall, it's also the snowiest, just barely edging out December. Then again, it's often clearer than December and November, as there are significantly fewer cloudy days. Plus, the days are getting longer. The gain in daylight really starts to be noticeable, too. By the end of the month, we gain about a full hour of daylight.

**What to Expect:** January may be cold and relatively clear, but in a weird way, this can be sort of refreshing. In my experience, one of the worst aspects of winter weather isn't cold or snow; it's the short days and the gloomy clouds that often characterize late fall and early winter. In January, things literally brighten up a bit.

With that said, don't let the beautiful light outside fool you; it can still be darn cold. So bundle up, then get out and enjoy the outdoors.

## February

HIGH: 28° ✳ LOW: 12° ✳ AVERAGE SNOWFALL: 7.7" (26.5" in 1962)

February is the shortest month of the year, but sometimes it feels like the longest. On average, February is a little warmer than January, but not by much, and it's also plenty snowy. This one-two punch gets old, and by February, you've already been subjected to this barrage for at least a few months. February can also get staggeringly cold; the coldest temperature ever recorded in Minnesota occurred on February 2, 1996, when the mercury hit -60 degrees below zero in Tower, Minnesota. In the Twin Cities, things were warmer, but not by all that much. The low still hit -32.

**What to Expect:** Honestly, February can be tough, but I find a bit of comfort in heaping abuse upon Punxsutawney Phil. Not only are his "predictions" wildly inaccurate, groundhogs also happen to live underground, where wind chill isn't a factor. (If that weren't bad enough, Phil even has better digs than that; he lives in the town's library with his wife, Phyllis.) The real trouble with Groundhog's Day is that its vague discussions of spring get your hopes up, and sometimes you may even get a nice February day, one that breaks 40 degrees (or even 50, though that's record-breaking territory). The next thing you know, you're planning picnics and imagining trips to the lake. Then, a few days or weeks later, the inevitable happens: it snows, or the temperature suddenly rivals that in Siberia. To put it mildly, there's a reason people take vacations in February and March. If you can't find a way to head south, consider planning some variety of staycation (see page 113).

## March

HIGH: 41° ✳ LOW: 24° ✳ AVERAGE SNOWFALL: 10.3" (40" in 1951)

March is a sight for sore eyes. While it can still get darn cold, the average temperature rises significantly; you'll no doubt find yourself positively giddy at the first trickle of 40-degree days.

Somewhat paradoxically, while March may be warmer than February, it gets significantly more snow, so don't pack away your shovels just yet.

**What to Expect:** While we still receive a good amount of snow in March (sometimes much more than the average), snow cover tends to wane somewhat. The snow that remains can be sloppy, as it has been subjected to repeated freezes and thaws. This can make snowmobiling, skiing and other outdoor activities difficult, if not impossible.

## April    HIGH: 57° ✻ LOW: 37° ✻ AVERAGE SNOWFALL: 2.4" (28.1" in 1983)

The poet T.S. Eliot knew what he was talking about when he wrote, "April is the cruelest month." After all, he was from the Midwest. On one hand, the last snow usually melts sometime in April, and this is surely cause for dancing in the streets. What's more, it can get outright warm! The grass might even green up! Then again, there is a reason that gardeners don't plant until mid-May. The weather is entirely capricious; it might snow one day and be 65 and sunny the next. Thankfully, the snow we get usually doesn't last all that long, though don't discount the possibility of a major spring storm. (In 2014, we had 19.5 inches the week before Easter.)

Now if a winter has been especially bad (a pox on your family, polar vortex!) any vestige of wintery weather may seem unbearable, but rest assured that even though you're likely to have some snow and a few chilly days, winter's on its last legs.

**What to Expect:** Get outside. April is the first month where you're likely to have a number of days on which you can hold a picnic or visit a park sans a parka. And while you'll definitely want to pack several layers of clothing in the car if you're braving the Twins home opener or a Minnesota United FC game, April is usually the month that breaks winter's back.

# Understanding Minnesota Winter
## It's a Big State!

Most of Minnesota's 5,400,000 people live in the Twin Cities metro area, but certainly not everyone does. Minnesota boasts such fine cities as Rochester, Duluth, St. Cloud and Moorhead, not to mention the countless towns and cities scattered across the state. On any given day, the state's climate varies significantly from north to south and east to west. At just smaller than the United Kingdom, Minnesota is a huge state, and it's therefore essential to note that the Twin Cities often have significantly different weather than that found outstate. Generally speaking, winter extremes/temperatures tend to be more pronounced up north; so while Minneapolis's record snowfall was the 28.4 inches from the 1991 Blizzard, that storm had nothing on the whopper that hit Finland, Minnesota, in 1994[1]. It dropped 46.5 inches of snow. Long story short, wherever you are in Minnesota, make sure to check the forecast!

360 miles from east to west

407 miles from north to south

## Length of Day

Although we're often referred to as "the North Country," Minnesota is only halfway to the North Pole. Still, we're far enough north that the length of our days varies a tremendous amount by season. This occurs because Earth is tilted on its axis, and the axis is pointed in a fixed direction (toward the North Star, as it happens[1]). Over great lengths of time, the axis slowly "wobbles," however, so the pole star varies over time. In 11,000 years or so, Vega—one of the brightest stars in the sky—will become the pole star.

This all means that the amount of light a location on Earth receives depends on its latitude. While Minnesota is nowhere near far enough north to experience the midnight sun (days when the sun never sets) or the downright terrifying polar night (days when the sun never rises), the length of our days varies plenty. Here's a rough guide to how much time you can expect between sunup and sundown.[1]

| MONTH | TOTAL DAYLIGHT ON THE 15TH | SUNRISE | SUNSET |
|---|---|---|---|
| January | 9 hr, 9 min. | 7:48 a.m. | 4:57 p.m. |
| March | 11 hr, 49 min. | 7:25 a.m. | 7:20 p.m. |
| June | 15 hr, 36 min. | 5:26 a.m. | 9:02 p.m. |
| September | 12 hr, 32 min. | 6:52 a.m. | 7:23 p.m. |
| December | 8 hr, 47 min. | 7:45 a.m. | 4:32 p.m. |

While our winter days get short, at least we don't have to deal with the polar night or the midnight sun (shown here in Norway)

**IT COULD BE WORSE** The shortest day of the year occurs on the winter solstice, which occurs on December 20, 21 or 22, depending on the year. On that day, Minneapolis-St. Paul sees just 8 hours and 46 minutes of daylight, barely enough to cover a full workday. (And if you head farther north, it gets a lot worse!) After that, we begin "gaining" daylight, which becomes readily noticeable by the time January rolls around (as we gain about an hour by the end of the month). These times don't count twilight, which occurs when the sun is below the horizon but light is scattered into the atmosphere.

## Growing Pains (the First/Last Frost)

As any Minnesota farmer can tell you, we have a relatively short growing season. In the Twin Cities area, the last frost usually occurs around May 10, and the first frost usually occurs between mid-to-late September and early October.[1] This means that our growing season is usually mid-May to late September.

## How Long is Snow on the Ground?

The short answer: Too long! In the Twin Cities, the first inch of snow usually shows up sometime in November and is gone by April. That doesn't mean it can't snow in April and May, though; on the contrary, it certainly can, although such spring snows usually don't last long. On average, the Twin Cities see about 100 days with an inch or more of snow on the ground; the winter of 1964-1965 saw an incredible 136 days of continuous snow cover, a full four and a half months![1]

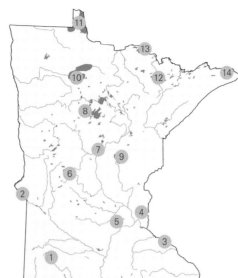

## Ice-out Dates

1. Shetek, April 5
2. Big Stone, April 9
3. Pepin, April 9
4. White Bear, April 12
5. Minnetonka, April 13
6. Osakis, April 16
7. Gull, April 21
8. Itasca, April 23

9. Mille Lacs, April 24
10. Lower Red, April 27
11. Lake of the Woods, April 29
12. Vermillion, April 29
13. Rainy, May 3
14. Gunflint, May 7

## Ice-in and Ice-out Dates

If you're interested in ice fishing, you might want to know when the lakes start to freeze. Minnesota is a huge state and the "ice-in" dates of the state's various lakes can differ a great deal by location (and by year).[1] With that said, lakes in the northern part of the state tend to freeze earlier—in mid-November—than lakes in the metro area or farther south, which tend to freeze in December. Because the data is somewhat spotty, it's not easy to find data for every lake.

While the "ice-in" data isn't the best, the records for ice-out dates are a lot better. Above are the average ice-out dates for some of the more popular lakes in the state.[2]

**Note:** Because not everyone agrees just what constitutes an ice-out. Some people insist that travel must be possible by boats; others say ice must be gone from 90 percent of the lake or more, etc.) so ice-out dates are actually pretty subjective. These dates are by no means absolute.

**IT COULD BE WORSE** When it comes to ice-out dates, some years are definitely worse than others. Snow showers during the fishing opener aren't unheard of, and on rare occasions, the lakes may not have iced out by the time the opener arrives. In 1966, Gunflint Lake didn't reach ice-out until May 26![1]

## Statewide Records

**Coldest Temperature on Record:** -60, Tower, 1996

**Most Snow in 24 hours:** 3 feet, Finland, Minnesota, 1994[1]

**Most Snow in an Entire Winter:** 170.5 inches, near Grand Portage, 1949[1]

**Deepest Snow on Record:** 88 inches, Meadowlands (near Cloquet), 1969[2]

**Lowest Wind Chill:** Perhaps -71 in northern Minnesota in January 1982, although this is not conclusive because of the sparse availability of wind data and temperature measurements across the state[3]

## Twin Cities Records

**Coldest Temperature on Record:** -34, January, 1936[1]

**Most Snow in 24 hours:** 21 inches, 1991[2]

**Most Snow in an Entire Winter:** 98.6 inches, 1983-1984[3]

**Deepest Snow on Record:** 38 inches, 1982[4]

**Lowest Wind Chill:** The wind chill may have reached -67 back in January of 1936[5]

*IT COULD BE WORSE* The winter of 1983-1984 produced a whopping 98.6 inches of snow in the Twin Cities.[1] That's 8 feet, 2 inches. Sometimes, we get lucky. The least snowy winter, in 1930-1931, produced a paltry 14.2 inches. By contrast, the average Twin Cities winter produces 47 inches of snow.[2]

## A Few of the Worst Blizzards in State History

### Schoolchildren's Blizzard

January 12, 1888 is a day that is still remembered across much of the Midwest. The day started out rather warm for January, but by the middle of the day, the temperature plummeted, snow began falling and the wind was howling. Students in one-room schoolhouses were sent home early, but many soon became lost in the storm's whiteout snow, and froze to death, sometimes just feet from safety. More than 230 people died in the blizzard.[1]

### Armistice Day Blizzard

Striking on a relatively warm November day in 1940, the Armistice Day Blizzard caught hundreds of Minnesotans unawares. The day started out relatively warmly, and given that duck hunting season was in full swing, many duck hunters took advantage of the nice weather to go hunting. As the day went on, it became clear that the hunting was very good—ducks streamed by in the thousands—but the weather was not. High winds and rain soon turned to high winds and snow, and hunters wearing warm-weather gear found themselves in an out-and-out blizzard. Many hunters were in duck boats on lakes or rivers when the full fury of the storm hit. With almost zero freeboard, these duck boats were no match for the five-foot waves produced by the storm's winds. Many hunters drowned; others attempted to take refuge on nearby shores or islands, where they had to endure temperatures in the single digits. Many didn't survive the night; in all, 49 Minnesotans died in the storm.

### Halloween Blizzard of 1991

When Minnesotans talk about blizzards, the Blizzard of 1991 is often a point of reference, and for good reason. In the Twin Cities, it was the snowiest blizzard on record; in fact, largely thanks to the Halloween Blizzard, as it is often known, November 1991 is the snowiest month in (recorded) history in Minneapolis-St. Paul. From October 31 to November 3, huge portions of the state saw over 2 feet of snow.[1] The snow was followed up by intense cold. Around 20 Minnesotans died in the storm, either in car crashes or because of heart attacks suffered while trying to shovel all of that snow.

## The Nation's Icebox?

Some parts of the state are renowned for their cold. On average, International Falls is the second-coldest National Weather Service station in the Lower 48, with a mean temperature of 37.4 degrees.[1] Only Mt. Washington in New Hampshire beats it, with a mean temp of 27.2. At an elevation of 6,288 feet, Mt. Washington is situated on a literal mountain. It's the windiest station that the National Weather Service operates and one of the windiest places in the world.[2] The top wind speed recorded is 231 miles per hour. International Falls, while cold, is not the coldest place in the state; it just is the coldest with a NOAA weather station. The coldest temperature ever recorded in Minnesota occurred in 1996 in Tower, Minnesota, although nearby Embarrass is constantly in the running for the "prize" of the coldest weather.

## Let's Be Real

Minnesota is a pretty cold place, but Alaskans are unimpressed by our winters, often describing them as "somewhat tame." And for all of our talk about living on the "frozen tundra"— a phrase I've used myself from time to time—we live about 700 miles from actual tundra.

 **IT COULD BE WORSE** The coldest recorded temperature in the continental U.S. was recorded in Rogers Pass, Montana, when it hit an astonishing -70 below; the U.S. record comes from Alaska, where the temp was just a shade above -80.[1]

## A Few Winter Pet Peeves

### What's with All the Static?

If you've never experienced a northern winter before, you might find yourself asking, what's with all the static? The problem boils down to humidity—if it's humid outside, electricity will dissipate naturally. Our winter is famous for being cold, but it's also quite dry. Dry air is an insulator, causing electricity to build up until we contact something conductive, and we feel the (painful) result. Thankfully, static is rarely dangerous though it can be a definite problem around

flammable materials, such as gasoline. (That's why you should never get back into your car when pumping gas.) If you're really bothered by static, there are several things you can do.[1] The first is run a humidifier in your house. The added moisture in the air makes it easier for the electricity to dissipate. Also, there are cans of antistatic spray that you can use on clothing.[2] Some fabrics are more static-prone than others; synthetic fabrics like nylon tend to be the worst. It's also easy to get zapped when you're entering your car. Before you get in, be sure to discharge the static by touching the metal on the car with another metal object (say, a key). This saves you pain from a static zap.[3]

**IT COULD BE WORSE** If you think the static is bad here, just imagine it in colder climates! In winter, Antarctica regularly reaches -70 degrees below zero and colder. When it's that cold, all the water in the air essentially freezes out, leading to incredibly low humidity levels—often in the single digits.[1] This makes static electricity a real hassle and a serious hazard when it comes to using electronic equipment (as the static has more than enough power to overload the very sensitive components inside).

## What Was That Thump?

When the cold weather really hits, you might hear some weird thumps or clunks in your house. No, your house doesn't have a ghost in it. Instead, the materials inside your house may simply be expanding or contracting—which often happens in exceedingly cold weather.[1] If the noise keeps up, however, or if you suspect your pipes or your roof are involved, don't hesitate to call in a professional to get things checked out.

## Preventing Chapped Lips

I'd be remiss not to mention one of the toughest areas to take care of in winter: your lips! Chapped lips are a major winter pain, and there is a relatively simple explanation behind them. When you go outside, moisture from your lips evaporates in the dry, cold air, drying out the skin. When you lick your lips, it actually makes things worse, as that moisture evaporates, making the skin drier than before.[1] That's why lip balm is often oil- or petroleum-based; the oil serves as a barrier between your lips and the elements.[2]

## Feel Gloomy Every Winter? It Could Be Seasonal Affective Disorder

When fall and winter roll around, many people report experiencing depression, which often lasts until spring arrives. What was once thought to be "the winter blues" is now known as a specific mental disorder: Seasonal Affective Disorder. The exact causes are unknown, but falling light levels are suspected to interfere with the body's internal clock, perhaps causing chemical imbalances in the body (and the brain). Seasonal Affective Disorder (known appropriately enough as S.A.D.) is more common the farther north you go, and approximately 10 percent of people in northern latitudes experience it.[1] Thankfully, treatments are available; light therapy is one popular treatment, as are doctor-prescribed medications. Given that S.A.D. is a recurring problem (many people experience it each year), it's important to visit a doctor if you suspect you have it.

**IT COULD BE WORSE** Of course, the falling light levels we face here in Minnesota are nothing compared to areas that experience polar night—total darkness for 24 hours. In such areas (the South Pole among them), this total lack of light throws off the body's internal clock, and oddly enough, this total lack of light makes it harder for folks to fall asleep (and stay sleeping). So why do I mention this? Well, just after the winter solstice, our days are mighty short, and it's likely you'll spend most of your days inside, under artificial light, without seeing much of the sun. This experience (especially when repeated) isn't all that different from the situation in the polar regions.[1]

## I Forgot to Pay My Heating Bill. Can They Turn My Heat Off? The Cold Weather Rule, Explained

Contrary to popular belief, if you don't pay your heating bill, your power company can shut off your heat in the winter; if you're having trouble paying the bills, you need to contact your utility company to invoke the Cold Weather Rule, a state rule that essentially limits the amount that power companies can charge low-income folks during the colder months. If your income is at or below 50 percent of the median average of the state median income, then you are not required to pay more than 10 percent of your monthly household income. The rule is in effect from October 15 to April 15. After April 15, you'll need to establish a payment plan with your utility company.

For a full run-down of the rule, visit http://mn.gov/puc/consumers/shut-off-protection/

# Understanding Weather Warnings and Watches[1]

Wherever you're spending time in Minnesota during the winter, you need to know the weather lingo; the National Weather Service issues specific warnings and watches to warn folks about different kinds of potentially dangerous winter weather. For the forecast, visit www.noaa.gov or www.weather.gov.

Before we get to the actual types of winter weather, it's important to know the difference between a weather warning and a watch. While both are serious (and should be heeded), there are major differences between the two.

**A Weather Warning** indicates that the phenomenon in question (a blizzard, say) is about to happen or is already in progress.[1]

**A Weather Watch** indicates that the conditions are right for the event to occur and that you should stay abreast of the forecast.[2]

Paying attention to weather warnings will let you know when to expect to see this outside

# The Details about Weather Warnings

## Winter Storm Warning[1]

This is exactly what it sounds like: a warning that a winter storm with heavy snow or ice buildup is occurring or about to happen. Generally speaking, in our area, a winter storm produces 4 or more inches of snow in 12 hours, or 6 or more inches in 24 hours. (Ice accumulation of more than a quarter of an inch also qualifies.)[2] Winter storms are hazardous and make driving and being outside treacherous and dangerous, if not outright impossible.

The definition of a winter storm varies by region, however; winter storm warnings are issued in southern states for storms that would merely serve to slow down your Minnesota morning commute.

## Blizzard Warning

While the term "blizzard" is often used somewhat loosely in everyday discussion, a blizzard has a specific meteorological definition. A storm is a blizzard if it has sustained winds or gusts of 35 miles per hour or more and falling/blowing snow that reduces visibility to less than a quarter mile for more than 3 hours.[3] Traveling in a blizzard is very dangerous, and the Department of Transportation often shuts down affected roads or sections of the interstate.

## Wind Chill Warning

Wind chill warnings are issued when the wind chill is deemed to be life threatening. While different areas define what a life-threatening wind chill is, it's usually in the ballpark of -35 or lower in Minnesota.[4]

# Understanding Weather Watches

## Winter Storm Watch
A winter storm may occur in the next 12 to 48 hours.[1]

## Winter Weather Advisory
Winter weather is on its way and will likely create significant inconveniences.[2] Translation: Travel is still possible, but you'll need to schedule more time for your commute and take things slowly to ensure safety.

## Wind Chill Advisory
Wind chill is expected to drop to potentially dangerous lows. While different areas define what a dangerous wind chill is, it's usually in the ballpark of -25 or lower in Minnesota.[3]

## Blizzard Watch
A blizzard may occur in the near future.[4]

## Lake Effect Snow Watch/Warning
Lake Effect snow occurs because large bodies of water (like the Great Lakes) cool more slowly than the surrounding air; when a mass of cold air passes over a warmer lake, it picks up water vapor, which freezes and falls as snow.[5] Such storms can produce an enormous amount of snow—think several feet in one storm—but thankfully, Lake Effect snow is much rarer in Minnesota than it is elsewhere (say, in Buffalo, New York). Lake Effect snow is usually restricted to Duluth and other cities on the North Shore, although some larger lakes (Mille Lacs) experience it to a lesser extent).

## What Is Wind Chill and Why Does It Matter?

Depending on whom you ask, wind chill is either worthless or really helpful. But before we get to that, what is it, exactly? Wind chill is an attempt to quantify how quickly the body loses heat when subjected to cold *and* wind.[1] Why is this important? Well, when it's windy and cold, the exposed skin loses heat faster than if it's just cold. This is important information to know, as it means that if it's below freezing and windy, frostbite can occur much faster.[2] If it's -25 and there's no wind, you might get frostbite in half an hour. If it's -25 and there's a 25 mile per hour wind, you could get it in 10 minutes or less. In this sense, wind chill is also an attempt to tell you how cold it will "feel" outside.

So what's the problem? Well, by definition, wind chill is a pretty subjective measure. The formula that determines wind chill has something of a one-size-fits-all approach. First off, the formula used to compute wind chill assumes that there is no impact from the sun; it assumes the person is outside at night. It also doesn't take individual metabolism into account or variations in height (which matters, because the face is one of the most commonly frostbitten areas), and it also doesn't take personal cold tolerance into account. (As the crazies who wear shorts when it's -20 make clear, some of us have a different cold tolerance than others.) In this writer's opinion, wind chill is useful for one primary reason: it alerts people to the danger that a combination of wind and cold pose, and that's why it seems prudent to peg school closures to wind chill, not air temperature. Still, I'll admit that wind chill's detractors have a point: for an essentially made-up measurement, wind chill gets a lot of airtime, certainly more than it deserves.

### Temperature (°F)[1]

| Wind (mph) | 40 | 35 | 30 | 25 | 20 | 15 | 10 | 5 | 0 | -5 | -10 | -15 | -20 | -25 | -30 | -35 | -40 | -45 |
|---|---|---|---|---|---|---|---|---|---|---|---|---|---|---|---|---|---|---|
| 5 | 36 | 31 | 25 | 19 | 13 | 7 | 1 | -5 | -11 | -16 | -22 | -28 | -34 | -40 | -46 | -52 | -57 | -63 |
| 10 | 34 | 27 | 21 | 15 | 9 | 3 | -4 | -10 | -16 | -22 | -28 | -35 | -41 | -47 | -53 | -59 | -66 | -72 |
| 15 | 32 | 25 | 19 | 13 | 6 | 0 | -7 | -13 | -19 | -26 | -32 | -39 | -45 | -51 | -58 | -64 | -71 | -77 |
| 20 | 30 | 24 | 17 | 11 | 4 | -2 | -9 | -15 | -22 | -29 | -35 | -42 | -48 | -55 | -61 | -68 | -74 | -81 |
| 25 | 29 | 23 | 16 | 9 | 3 | -4 | -11 | -17 | -24 | -31 | -37 | -44 | -51 | -58 | -64 | -71 | -78 | -84 |
| 30 | 28 | 22 | 15 | 8 | 1 | -5 | -12 | -19 | -26 | -33 | -39 | -46 | -53 | -60 | -67 | -73 | -80 | -87 |
| 35 | 28 | 21 | 14 | 7 | 0 | -7 | -14 | -21 | -27 | -34 | -41 | -48 | -55 | -62 | -69 | -76 | -82 | -89 |
| 40 | 27 | 20 | 13 | 6 | -1 | -8 | -15 | -22 | -29 | -36 | -43 | -50 | -57 | -64 | -71 | -78 | -84 | -91 |
| 45 | 26 | 19 | 12 | 5 | -2 | -9 | -16 | -23 | -30 | -37 | -44 | -51 | -58 | -65 | -72 | -79 | -86 | -93 |
| 50 | 26 | 19 | 12 | 4 | -3 | -10 | -17 | -24 | -31 | -38 | -45 | -52 | -60 | -67 | -74 | -81 | -88 | -95 |
| 55 | 25 | 18 | 11 | 4 | -3 | -11 | -18 | -25 | -32 | -39 | -46 | -54 | -61 | -68 | -75 | -82 | -89 | -97 |
| 60 | 25 | 27 | 10 | 3 | -4 | -11 | -19 | -26 | -33 | -40 | -48 | -55 | -62 | -69 | -76 | -84 | -91 | -98 |

Wind (miles per hour)

**Frostbite Times:** 30 minutes   10 minutes   5 minutes

## Wind Chill Facts

### Wind Chill Temperatures Don't Reflect the Air Temperature

The wind chill temperatures bandied about by meteorologists aren't, in any sense, real. If the thermometer reads -20, it's -20. Wind speed—no matter if it's 5 miles per hour or 50—doesn't affect the temperature. So if you're bragging to out-of-towners about surviving a wind chill of -30 (we've all done it!), keep in mind that this isn't the lowest temperature you've ever experienced.

### Wind Chill Doesn't Affect Objects

If it's twenty below, your car may not start, but don't blame the wind. Because wind chill is designed to measure heat loss from warm-blooded people and animals, applying it to cars and other objects doesn't make sense.[1] The wind chill is as irrelevant to a car as blood pressure. Wind chill does apply to other animals, however; this includes household pets, so if the wind chill drops, be sure to look after your furry friends.

### If It's Not Below Freezing, You Can't Get Frostbite, No Matter the Wind Chill

This bears repeating: Wind speed doesn't affect the air temperature. As its name implies, frostbite requires freezing temperatures—air temps of 32 or below. If the air temp is above 32, you usually can't get frostbite. (There's one exception: if your skin cools down in part because of evaporative cooling—essentially moisture evaporating from your skin. This, in theory, could cause frostbite at temperatures above 32 degrees, but unless you're driving in an open convertible when it's 33 degrees, it's pretty unlikely.)[2]

### Wind Chill Isn't the Only Winter Weather Danger; Hypothermia Kills

It doesn't have to be particularly cold for you to develop hypothermia, which occurs when the body's temperature drops below 95 degrees. According to the Mayo Clinic, even seemingly "mild" temperatures (say, at or around freezing) can lead to hypothermia, especially if you stay out in the weather too long (say, after passing out on the way home from a night at the tavern).[3] Over the course of 2006 to 2010, an average of 358 people died per year because of the cold in the Midwest.[4] In Minnesota, we have about 20-some cold-related deaths per year.[5]

**_IT COULD BE WORSE_** In the Arctic and Antarctica, people really see air temps of -45 and lower, and they have more than enough wind, too. As of this writing, it's a balmy -43 at the South Pole, with wind speeds of 17 miles per hour.[1] That's good for a wind chill of -76. In the worst Antarctic weather, hurricane-force winds aren't uncommon, and neither are incredibly cold temperatures. You put those together, and you get maximum wind chills in the range of -150, maybe lower.

# Wintertime Meteorological Phenomena

There's more to winter than wind chill and short days. It also produces some stunning weather phenomena, and upon closer inspection, even garden-variety phenomena, such as the humble snowflake, are surprisingly complex. Here's a brief run-down of some of the more interesting winter weather phenomena that Minnesota has to offer.

## Snow

We rarely pay much more attention to snow than is needed to shovel the stuff off the driveway, but when you look closer, there's a lot to see! Snow consists of ice crystals of varying shapes— not all snowflakes are the characteristic star-like shape you recognize from childhood. There are actually dozens of forms that snowflakes can take, and these include column-like shapes, plane-like shapes and a variety of other options.[1]

Whatever shape they take, snowflakes all form in the same way. Water vapor in a cloud condenses into ice and begins forming a hexagonal crystal. This crystal grows and branches out.[2] Over time, the crystal moves around the cloud, where it experiences changes in temperature and humidity. This affects the snowflake's ultimate shape.

By the time they reach the ground, many snowflakes aren't symmetrical, and some are less than pretty. And by the time they reach the ground, they often consist of a number of different crystals that have clumped together.[3] This means that there is a lot to find on your average snowflake hunt.

## Different Types of Snow and Ice

**Snow** consists of hexagonal ice crystals; a snowflake can either be a single crystal or a collection of several crystals

**Sleet** consists of almost grain-like ice pellets that originate from frozen raindrops or partially melted, refrozen snowflakes. When sleet hits the ground, it usually bounces.[1]

**Freezing Rain** falls as rain, but immediately freezes into a layer of ice when it hits the ground.[2]

**A Flurry** is a brief snow shower; flurries don't produce much more than a dusting of snow.

**Graupel** is the odd duck of winter precipitation; it forms when water becomes supercooled (cooled below 32 degrees, but remains liquid) and then merges with a snow crystal, which causes it to solidify into a white pellet.[3] When graupel hits the ground, it doesn't bounce so much as splat, like a tiny snowball.

**Slush** is snow that has partially melted after contacting the ground, which is warmer than freezing.

**Black Ice** forms when the air temperature is warmer than the pavement temperature.[1] Moisture from the warm air freezes on the pavement, creating a thin, transparent (and often invisible) layer of ice. Black ice is infamous for causing crashes, and it often forms on bridges, overpasses, tunnels and other areas that cool more quickly (because they are exposed to more air circulation). Snowplows in Minnesota disperse salt, which lowers the freezing point of water, and this can help melt the ice (as long as the temperatures don't drop too low).

**Frost** is a thin layer of ice crystals that forms when moisture condenses directly into ice.[1] Hard frost (also known as a killing frost) causes the water in plants to freeze; depending on how thoroughly a plant is affected, some parts of the plant can be damaged, or the entire organism can die.[2] See page 15 for a rough guide to the first/last frost.

**Surface Hoar Frost** is something you're familiar with even if you don't realize it. It's often what gives morning snowbanks their dazzling sparkle.[1] It forms because of temperature changes during the day/night. During the day, the snow heats up, some water in the snow evaporates, and frost then crystallizes on the surface.

**Hoarfrost** is essentially surface hoar frost that has grown to a large size; just as rock crystals (say, quartz) can sometimes grow to very large sizes, ice crystals can, too, if the conditions are right. It forms when it's quite cold and there's a source of water vapor (such as a river, say) nearby.[1] (It also helps if the area is undisturbed and sheltered from wind.)

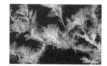

**Eskimo Words for Snow:** There's a long-standing myth that there are so-and-so words for snow in the "Eskimo" language. Some say 50, some say 100. The trouble is, it's not true. There are actually 6 different "Eskimo" languages, and the blanket term is often used to refer to all indigenous folks who live in the Far North, either in Canada, Alaska or Greenland.[1] When it comes to the number of "snow" terms, it varies by language (and how you define/count the terms).[2] Surprisingly enough, no one bothered to consult experts in the actual languages until relatively recently. The result? It depends on what you count, but there are about two dozen words in Inupiaq (spoken in Northern Canada) related to snow.[3] That may be more than in some languages, but it's a far cry from the totals alleged in popular culture.

### A Few (unofficial) Types of Snow

Still, there is a germ of truth to the "many words for snow" claim. When you spend a good portion of your time amid the ice and snow, it's only natural to carefully analyze and carefully categorize the weather phenomena you see. This is true in the Arctic and in Minnesota. Like skiers and snowboarders, your average Minnesotan often refers to a number of unofficial terms for snow. While this list is by no means definitive, it'll give you a leg-up if you're from more tropical climes.

**Powdery, Fluffy or Thin Snow** is generally dry snow that forms under cold, dry conditions. It's great for skiing and snowboarding and easy to shovel (as long as feet of it don't fall), but it's lousy for snowmen. (Despite all the ice and the cold, much of Antarctica is therefore relatively lousy for making snowmen.) Sadly for snowboarders and such, powder doesn't stick around for all that long, as it can quickly become packed down or its surface melts, producing a "crusty" top layer.

**"Crusty"** snow forms when snow falls, then its top layer melts and re-freezes; this creates a crust of snow. Sometimes this crust is strong enough to hold your weight, but sometimes it holds for a second before giving way and sending your leg into the snow. Crusty snow usually isn't great for snowmen and the like, but it can be a lot of fun for outdoor adventurers, especially snowshoers. Trudging through it also makes for a good (albeit strenuous!) winter hike.

**Icy Snow** results when snow is packed down quite a bit and then its surface freezes; it can also form when the top layer of snow freezes and refreezes enough to create a glazed-like surface; icy snow is the bane of many skiers.

**Thick, Sticky Snow** forms when it's warmer but still cold enough to freeze the snow. It's great for snowmen but terrible to shovel and not ideal for many outdoor pursuits (including snowmobiling).

**Slushy Snow** consists of snow that has partially, but not entirely, melted. By definition, you need temperatures around freezing (often just warmer) to produce slush. Slush is heavy stuff; in my experience, it's the worst kind of snow to shovel. Slush season marks the end of many wintertime activities (as it often leaves you sopping wet).

**Late Season Snow** falls, then almost immediately disappears once on the ground. This occurs when the air temperature is just cold enough to produce snow, but the ground temperature is warm enough to melt the snow immediately (or soon thereafter). A common sight in late spring, it's not unusual to receive three or four inches of snow overnight only to find it gone (or mostly so) by the next evening. If it snows late enough in the season, you might not even need to shovel.

## Wet Snow vs. Dry Snow

Just as snowflakes differ quite a bit—the old adage about no two snowflakes is mostly true—the same goes for the snow that each storm produces.[1] In fact, one of the first things you'll probably hear after a big storm is talk about how "wet" or "dry" the snow is. This might strike you as confusing, given that all snow consists of the same stuff (ice crystals).

While snowflakes have the same base material (ice), they don't always have the same amounts of it. As anyone who has lugged around a five-gallon water container can tell you, water is some seriously heavy stuff. Dry, powdery snow generally forms when it's colder, when there is less moisture left in the air, so dry, powdery snow is light because it contains less water.

When it's warmer, there's often more moisture in the air, so when flakes form, they tend to stick together. This is what gives the big flakes in our March and April storms such a striking size and weight; instead of consisting of one single flake, they often consist of many individual crystals, and they are chock full of water, making them heavy. Warmer temps make snow "stickier" because the ice crystals can melt and re-freeze, sticking back together.[2] (You can create this effect by clumping together a bunch of snow in your bare hand. This melts it, and it sticks together once it re-freezes.)

33

# How Much Water is in All That Snow?

As a general rule, 10 inches of snow is equivalent to one inch of liquid.[1] This can vary significantly, however, depending on the temperature in the atmosphere when the snow forms. Light, powdery snow forms at relatively cold temperatures, so it doesn't contain much water, but it can sure pile up, as it's less dense. That's why Lake Effect snow (which consists of light, powdery snow) takes up so much darn room: A relatively small amount of water produces a lot of snow, sometimes feet and feet of the stuff. In comparison, if the atmospheric temperature is around freezing, then the snow contains a lot more water, and that water is packed much more densely, producing a smaller amount of thick, heavy snow.

The basic rule of thumb is simple: Low atmospheric temperature = many inches of dry, powdery snow. Warmer atmospheric temperatures = far less accumulation, but thicker, heavy flakes.

For example, at around 0 degrees, one inch of water produces a whopping 40 inches of snow. At around freezing, the same amount produces only 10 (but 10 inches of snow you certainly wouldn't want to shovel).[2]

Similarly, under the right circumstances (say, a polar front over a still-warm Great Lake), snow can form when it's well below zero, producing a huge amount of snow. At -20 and lower, an inch of water would produce 100 inches of dry, powdery snow. At around freezing, it'd produce 10 inches of snow.[3]

| MELTWATER EQUIVALENT (IN.) | TEMPERATURE (°F) / NEW SNOWFALL (IN.)[1] | | | | | | |
|---|---|---|---|---|---|---|---|
| | 34 to 28 | 27 to 20 | 19 to 15 | 14 to 10 | 9 to 0 | 1 to -20 | -21 to -40 |
| .05 | .05 | .08 | 1.0 | 1.5 | 2.0 | 2.5 | 5.0 |
| .10 | 1.0 | 1.5 | 2.0 | 3.0 | 4.0 | 5.0 | 10.0 |
| .20 | 2.0 | 3.0 | 4.0 | 6.0 | 8.0 | 10.0 | 20.0 |
| .50 | 5.0 | 7.5 | 10.0 | 15.0 | 20.0 | 25.0 | 50.0 |
| 1.00 | 10.0 | 15.0 | 20.0 | 30.0 | 40.0 | 50.0 | 100.0 |
| 2.00 | 20.0 | 30.0 | 40.0 | 60.0 | 80.0 | 100.0 | 200.0 |

# Rarer Winter Phenomena

For all the hardships it imposes, a northern winter also offers some absolutely wonderful weather quirks, including everything from halos and arcs to thundersnow and sun pillars. Many of the most familiar wintertime optical phenomena are caused by ice—what else? Specifically, they are caused by ice crystals in the atmosphere; these crystals act as prisms and refract light, causing it to change direction somewhat. The effects produced depend on the shape of the crystals, their orientation and how much they divert the light, making sun dogs and the like essentially an atmospheric geometry problem.

## Sun Dogs and Halos

Sun dogs occur when sunlight refracts after passing through hexagonal ice crystals that are oriented horizontally. These serve as a prism and divert the light by about 22 degrees, causing two bright spots to appear to observers on the same plane.[1] One sun dog (or mock sun, as they are often called) is found on each side of the

sun, and each is about 22 degrees away from the sun. "22 degree halos" occur for the same reason as sun dogs; the only difference is that the hexagonal ice crystals are randomly oriented, causing the light to be refracted uniformly—in a circle with a radius of 22 degrees.[2] (This phenomenon can be seen with the moon as well.) If the conditions are right, you can see sun dogs and the 22 degree halo (and sometimes even additional halos) at the same time. Sun dogs and halos are sometimes seen with an often "winged" arc at the top—this is called the tangent arc and forms when columnar ice crystals serve as prisms, causing the light to refract at a different angle, producing a different optical effect.[3]

## Sun Pillars

Sun pillars are another rare treat. Seen at sunrise or sunset, they occur when hexagonal ice crystals falling from clouds high in the atmosphere catch the sun's light. This produces a "pillar" of light that actually consists of light reflected from millions of individual crystals.[1] Sun pillars can change over time (sometimes lengthening or brightening), so if you see one, keep an eye on it.

## The Luck of the Draw

Of course, you don't always see each of these effects—sometimes you'll see sun dogs and a halo, but no tangent arc, and at other times you might see sun dogs, but less crisp or clear examples. For these effects to occur, the atmospheric conditions have to be right. There have to be ice crystals, and they have to be just the right shape and oriented in the right way. Some days are just better than others. Not surprisingly, these phenomena are more common farther north, where there are more opportunities for the right conditions to form. What's more, the phenomena described above aren't the only types you can see. There are a number of others. For a full run-down, visit the wonderful site Atmospheric Optics (www.atoptics.co.uk/halo/unusual.htm)

## Mirages

Almost everyone's familiar with the sight of a mirage over a highway on a hot day. But it'd be a mistake to call them optical illusions; mirages are real phenomena caused by conditions in the atmosphere.[1] Specifically, they occur when there are temperature differences in adjacent layers of air. Because they are "real" in this sense, that's why you can photograph them! (In comparison, that full moon that positively looks huge on the horizon? That's an illusion; just try taking a picture of it or placing your thumb over it.) Mirages occur because air density changes with temperature—cold air is denser than warm air—and the air's density determines how much it refracts, or bends, light. (Cold air refracts light more than warm air does.)

So how does this figure into our winters? Well, while we're most familiar with "inferior mirages" that occur when hot areas (highways) are overlain by cooler air, the state (especially near Lake Superior) is also home to "superior mirages."

Superior mirages are much rarer, and occur when a layer of cold air near the surface is overlain by a layer of warm air. (This is called a temperature inversion; usually, the higher up you go, the colder things get.) Because cold air refracts light more than warm air, this sometimes produces an absolutely staggering sight: landscapes (and even cities and ships!) appear to float above the horizon.[2] Because superior mirages are so rare, they are often baffling to first-time viewers, leading to all sorts of speculation about their cause.

---

**Strange but True:** Superior mirages can confuse even trained explorers. While attempting to discover the Northwest Passage in 1818, Sir John Ross "discovered" a mountain range he called the Croker Mountains.[1] The mountains turned out to be a superior mirage; one of his crew members (who had protested the decision not to investigate the mountains further) led his own expedition a year later and sailed right over the alleged "mountains."

# Special Treats

**Rime** isn't actually a type of frost, per se; it occurs when water droplets in a cloud collide with snow crystals (often coating them). When they are coated entirely, it's referred to as graupel.[1] Usually, however, when folks refer to rime, they're talking about the neat "rime frost" crystals they wake up to find draped over everything.

There are two types of rime frost: soft rime, which produces tender, fragile, needle-like crystals, and hard rime, which is thicker and tougher. Both types of rime frost form in a similar way thanks to the presence of supercooled water.[1] The details of supercooling are a bit confusing, but a construction metaphor can tell you the basics: Water doesn't always freeze when it reaches 32 degrees. Freezing is somewhat akin to construction. When a crystal solidifies, it builds a (literal) structure. When water (including rime droplets) is supercooled, there isn't much of a structure for the ice to build on; it needs a framework. Rime frost (hard or soft) occurs when supercooled water droplets (usually in the form of fog or mist) find just such a framework, either a preexisting ice crystal or a frozen surface. When that happens, blammo, it freezes on contact. The result? Some some absolutely wonderful sights.[3]

---

**Strange but True:** While supercooling may seem a bit out there, it's a common survival tactic among polar animals; some fish species spend much of their lives in a supercooled state. They can survive this way because they literally have a type of antifreeze in their blood and because they avoid contact with ice. If exposed to ice, they "flash freeze" and often die. This usually doesn't happen in nature, but scientists have confirmed it can occur in the lab. One paper on the subject was titled "An Experimental Study of the Death of Supercooled Fish Resulting from Contact with Ice."[1]

## Sastrugi

Have you ever seen a snowbank that has been carved by the wind?[1] These formations are often associated with polar regions where they are quite common and can make travel over snow incredibly difficult. You can find them in Minnesota, too, but here they are more of a natural curiosity for most folks than anything else.

## Thundersnow

Thundersnow is (literally) what it sounds like: a snowstorm accompanied by thunder. Such storms are rare because thunder is caused by lightning, and for lightning to be present you usually need two things: moisture and instability.[1] As winter is drier and more atmospherically stable than summer, lightning is more common in summer storms. But it's not impossible in winter storms; if there's a ready moisture source (say, the Great Lakes) and instability (two different weather fronts meeting), then snow (or sleet) can fall, accompanied by lightning and thunder. It's rare—I've lived in Minnesota for most of my life and have only heard it two times—but it does happen.

# Winter on the Big Lake
## November Gales

Lake Superior (and the other Great Lakes) produces its own wintertime effects. For example, the infamous Gales of November (one of which sunk the *Edmund Fitzgerald*) are caused by the combination of cold fall air moving over the still relatively warm lake waters. This is the perfect recipe for instability and, often, large storms.

## The Lake Effect

Lake Effect snow is another well-known wintertime effect produced by the Big Lake. When very cold air sweeps down from Canada, it often encounters open water, where it picks up enough moisture to produce feet and feet of light, powdery snow. This makes the Great Lakes some of the largest snowmakers on Earth, and in some storms, five inches of snow per hour can fall.[1] Lake Effect storms aren't one-off deals, either. Some winters produce many independent storms. In the winter of 2014-2015, nearly 21 feet(!) of snow fell in an area near Buffalo, New York.[2] Lake Effect storms are really hit-or-miss; however, when the snow falls, it falls quickly, so areas that are relatively close together can see vastly different totals. Lake Effect storms are only a threat when the moisture source—the lakes—are unfrozen; once the lakes freeze up, Lake Effect snow is no longer a threat.

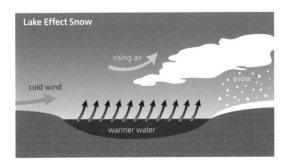

Lake Effect Snow

rising air

snow

cold wind

warmer water

Thankfully, the prevailing weather patterns tend to send weather systems away (rather than toward) our portions of Lake Superior, so while our parts of Superior provide the moisture for Lake Effect snow, it gets deposited in Wisconsin and Michigan. This isn't always the case, however. Lake Effect storms can hit the North Shore, and the effect is also present (to a much smaller extent) near our other large lakes, including Mille Lacs.

## Lake Superior Freezing Over

Every winter, ice forms on Lake Superior, but ice cover varies greatly by year, and the lake rarely freezes over.[1] (Even then, the lake isn't totally frozen over, as some spots resist freezing.) When a big freeze happens, however, it's a sight to see, and it leads to some amazing photo opportunities—including at the ice caves in Bayfield, Wisconsin. (I know, I know, this is a book about Minnesota, but I'd be remiss not to mention this amazing—and rare—travel opportunity). Because lake ice is inherently dangerous, National Park officials only give the OK for tourists to trek across the ice every few years (and even then, only for a short window of time).

Even if you don't venture on the ice, seeing the lake in winter is interesting, as the ice cover completely transforms the beaches. What's more, once spring rolls around, the shipping season begins to rev up, and you'll eventually see Coast Guard ice breakers assisting freighters in the area. In especially severe winters, you'll see Coast Guard vessels leading convoys of freighters through the leads in the ice.

## Ice Tsunamis

Every few years, Minnesota makes the news because of so-called "ice tsunamis."[1] If you've seen the videos online, you can understand why. A wall of ice slowly makes its way onto land, wrecking cabins, outbuildings, whatever it hits. The term itself is more than a bit misleading—they aren't tsunamis at all. Instead, there's a much simpler explanation: wind. Strong winds, if they are consistent enough, can push lake ice onshore, and once the ice gets going, it's impossible to stop it.

## What about the Polar Vortex?

The much-ballyhooed buzzword of the 2014 winter, the polar vortex is actually something of a technical weather term that refers to an air system that is usually hovering above the northern polar region.[1] Sometimes, however, the system shifts significantly southward, giving us weather that polar bears are more accustomed to. This actually happens when the vortex system weakens—not strengthens—and the jet stream (which is usually separate) distributes the cold air where it's (definitely!) unwanted.[2]

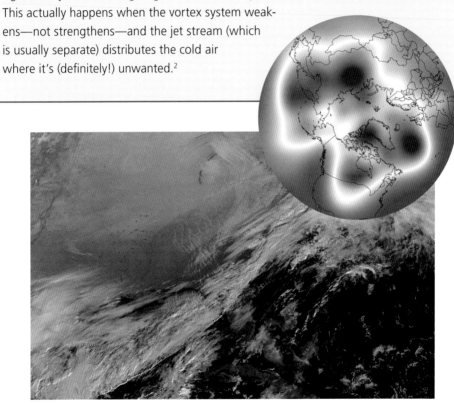

# Before the First Storm Hits:
# Cry a Little, Then Get Prepared

Preparing for winter should start in the fall, not a few days before the first storm is slated to hit. Winterproofing helps you save money, stay warm and can even help keep you and your loved ones alive.

## Assemble a Winter Emergency Kit[1]

I'm no doomsday prepper, but when severe weather hits, it's always best to have an emergency kit. This is especially true in winter, as you really don't want to be stuck without heat if the power goes out or without supplies if you get snowed in. So before winter hits, make sure your emergency kit is ready to go.

Nonperishable food and water for your family

Warm clothes, blankets and gear to help you withstand the cold

A NOAA weather radio and a portable radio, with batteries

A cell phone and a charger

An alternative heat source—if using propane, read the owner's manual and have a carbon monoxide detector nearby

Snow removal gear, including extra shovels

Household tools

A well-stocked first aid kit, medical supplies, and extra medication

Don't forget your pet! Stock up on pet food and medical supplies

Car adapters for your cell phone (and for other electrical devices)

A car with a full gas tank

Games and books for kids, as well as portable media devices

A generator (if you really expect to be snowed in)

For more information visit
www.ready.gov or www.noaa.gov

# Tune Up Your Furnace or Heating Element

When it gets cold, you need to stay warm, so it's important to ensure that your heating source is tuned-up and ready to go. A poorly maintained heating source can lead to carbon monoxide poisoning. Carbon monoxide is an odorless, invisible gas that's a by-product of incomplete combustion. In an average year in the U.S., about 430 deaths occur because of carbon monoxide poisoning, about 14 of whom die in Minnesota.[1,2] Because carbon monoxide is a by-product of heating elements, it's no surprise that most carbon monoxide deaths occur in the winter.

## Symptoms of Carbon Monoxide Poisoning Include

- Headache
- Dizziness
- Confusion
- Upset stomach and/or vomiting
- Coma, followed by death

## To Avoid Issues with Carbon Monoxide

Have your furnace tuned-up and inspected yearly; the same goes if you use wood-burning stoves or have a fireplace, as the chimney/flue must be cleaned and the masonry must be checked to ensure it is free from cracks.[3]

Do not use propane heaters or other portable combustion-based heaters indoors.

Install carbon monoxide detectors near each bedroom. These are relatively cheap, but they can be real lifesavers.

If you warm your car up in the morning (you should!), pull your car out of an attached garage. Leaving it in the garage (even with the door open) can sometimes cause carbon monoxide to enter a house (especially if the wind blows the wrong way).

Carbon monoxide poisoning can also occur in vehicles, including those that are running and stuck in snow.[4]

Be careful about using combustion-powered heaters and drinking alcohol at the same time; intoxication makes you less likely to recognize the symptoms of carbon monoxide poisoning.

If the power's out, some combustion-based heaters are marketed as "indoor safe." These feature internal oxygen sensors and turn off if the oxygen reaches a dangerous level; they also burn very efficiently.[5] For this reason, they make a good "emergency heater," but you still must heed the manufacturer's instructions and use great caution with them.[6] An oversized heater, if used in an enclosed space, can still cause a serious problem, and even a small heater, when used in a tent or another enclosed space, can be dangerous, especially if the symptoms of carbon monoxide poisoning go undetected (e.g., if someone is sleeping). If you decide to use one, keep in mind that they aren't foolproof, so be sure to keep a carbon monoxide detector nearby.[7]

Never use a gas oven to heat a home temporarily.

If you suspect carbon monoxide poisoning (or your carbon monoxide detector goes off), seek access to fresh air immediately and call 911.

# Winterizing Inside the House

Once you have your heating source tuned up and ready to go, it's time to winterproof your residence. This will help you save on your heating bills and can also prevent damage to your house (and even prevent fires).

## Winter Fire Safety

One of the first things to consider when waterproofing your house isn't cold—it's fire. Many house fires occur in winter. If you take the following precautions you can lessen the risk of a fire.

First of all, make sure you have ready access to fire extinguishers (and check that they are up to date and ready to go); make sure your residence has smoke detectors with fresh batteries.[1]

Clean out your vents for your dryer, furnace, oven and fireplace (as applicable); if vents are blocked, they can easily lead to a fire. This is especially true for dryers—just how flammable is dryer lint? It's a perfect ingredient for DIY fire starters.

Be incredibly careful about using supplemental electrical heaters. They are a nice way to warm up a room, but they also spark many house fires. If you use one, be sure there is nothing flammable nearby and that it has a sensor that turns it off if it tips over.

If the lights go out, opt for a flashlight instead of candles.

If you have a live Christmas tree, be sure to keep it well-watered. Dry Christmas trees can literally burst into flames when exposed to a source of flame.

Finally, make sure your windows aren't blocked by snow; you might need to use them to get out of a fire.

## Winterizing Doors and Windows

It should come as no surprise that most drafts enter a house from windows and doors, so winterizing these troublesome areas is a great way to save on energy bills. There are many ways winterize these trouble spots. Here are a few of the most popular.

### Caulking Gaps in Windows and Doors

Caulking windows and doors physically seals any gaps between your window frame or door and the actual window/door itself. This literally stops a draft in its tracks. Caulking is pretty easy to do, and relatively inexpensive. All you need is a caulking "gun" and the caulk itself. The gun helps squeeze out the caulk (although manual caulk

tubes are available as well). The caulk fits into the gap between the window and the frame, and you just smooth out the caulk with a wet finger. (Then just clean up any excess.) If you haven't ever done it, don't fret, there are many fine explanations on YouTube and the like. Best of all, the total cost is low—around $20—and it can lead to significant energy savings.

### Using Window Film

A common sight inside many homes in winter, window film is used to cover the interior of a house window in order to add an additional barrier between your window and your house.

If you've never done this, you're essentially shrink-wrapping the interior of your window. Window film kits vary in size, and usually contain a folded plastic film, and sticky tape. You attach the tape to the window frame, then adhere the plastic sheet to it, so the entire shebang covers the window. This creates an initial barrier to any drafts in the area. Then, you're going to need a blow dryer. That's not a joke. Applying hot air to the plastic causes it to shrink, making the seal on the window more complete. If you've never done this, you'll definitely feel weird blow-drying your windows, but believe me, it's worth it. When we did it, areas that were previously draft-prone often become markedly warmer. (I'm looking at you, living room window in my house!)

## Weather Sealing Strips

Weather sealing is another option; these rubber/plastic/foam strips adhere to the window or door frame, and this barrier helps keep out drafts. Weather sealing strips vary by the type of door or window you have, so make sure to measure your door/window before you head to the store. In addition, the sealing strips often have to be installed in a specific direction (some varieties have a "V" that point in that direction), so be sure to read the instructions. When in doubt, ask someone at a hardware store for help; believe me, it's a question they probably receive all too often. In my experience, stay away from the cheap foam products, as they don't adhere all that well; also be very careful when removing these strips, as they can cause damage to paint and trim.

## High-efficiency Windows/Doors and Upgrading Insulation

If you own your residence, another option is replacing your existing windows with more efficient models or storm windows.[1] This is especially important if you have an old house, as older windows are often less efficient. Selecting the right energy-efficient window can be a bit tricky and requires some homework, as you need to take into account the direction a window faces, the window's composition (and that of the frame), and the various types of coatings available on modern windows (as they vary in terms of the amount of light they let in and so on).[2] Still, if you've got a drafty house, the long-term savings often make it worthwhile, especially if you can afford to replace the windows in the entire house.

## Preventing Frozen Pipes

When water pipes freeze, ice forms and expands, sometimes causing pipes to burst. This can create a heck of a mess, but thankfully burst pipes are relatively easy to prevent.

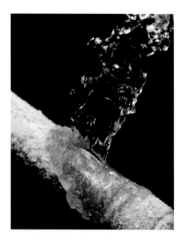

If you leave for an extended amount of time, keep your thermostat at or above 55 degrees.

When it gets really cold, keep an eye on areas that don't receive a great deal of heat—the pipes under your bathroom or kitchen sink, for example. Opening cabinet doors can help increase airflow.

Keep your faucets a bit open; running water freezes more slowly than stagnant water; this wastes some water, but it can help prevent ice formation.

If your house or building has pipes that are in an unheated area of the house, you'll either need to insulate those areas or add pipe insulation. (To my eye, they look a bit like sweaters that wrap around the pipe).[1]

Freezing pipes are also possible in areas of the house that are under-insulated; if one of your walls has water damage or mold, check its insulation. It may be under-insulated, and you may need to upgrade the insulation to protect the pipes.[2]

If you're going on vacation, have someone check on your house if a storm hits while you're away; if the power's out, your heat probably is too, and your pipes may freeze.

## Unfreezing A Pipe

If a pipe is leaking or has burst, the first thing you need to do is to turn off your water, so be sure to know where your water shutoff valve is before winter hits. Then it's time to call a plumber.

If you suspect a pipe has frozen but it isn't leaking and hasn't burst, you may be able to unfreeze it.

First, turn on a faucet connected to that pipe; if no water comes out or if it produces only a trickle of water, you might have frozen pipes; if you suspect you do, go to your water shutoff valve and turn off the water.[1] To unfreeze a pipe, you need to apply gradual heat. Like most materials, water expands when heated; water's odd in that it also expands when it's frozen. This is why using open-flame sources (like a blowtorch) to heat a frozen pipe is a bad idea; it's likely to cause your pipes to burst and can even create pockets of steam. To put it simply: Steam + bursting pipes + open flames = a recipe for a disaster.[2] Also, many pipes consist of plastic or PVC, so open flame sources will simply melt the pipes. Similarly, don't pour hot/boiling water down the drain; this can cause the same types of problems.

Instead, once you find where a pipe is frozen, the best way to go about warming up a frozen pipe is by using gradual heat. Wrapping pipes in warm towels often works, and a portable heater is another option, but always be careful about using electric equipment near wet areas, as this can be an electrocution hazard.

When in doubt, contact a plumber; if you think that some of your pipes are likely to freeze, it's a heck of lot easier to be proactive in the fall and get advice from an expert before winter hits.

## Upgrading Insulation

Replacing (or upgrading) insulation is another way to ensure that your house is energy efficient. Choosing the right insulation can be tricky, but the basics are easy to understand: Insulation is rated according to its R-value.[1] The higher the R-value, the more efficient the insulation is. Not all areas of a house have the same type of insulation; attics need heavy-duty insulation (because heat rises), whereas other areas (say, basement crawlspaces) need less, as there is less heat to retain.

There are many varieties of insulation, some of which are easy to install (such as the well-known fiberglass insulation) and others that need to be installed by a professional (spray-on foam insulation). Upgrading insulation is a good idea if you've got an older house (1980s and before), but it's worth looking into even if your house is newer, as upgraded insulation can cut heating and cooling bills significantly.[2]

## Find Other Drafts

An infrared temperature "gun" is a great tool to get while you're weatherproofing. Essentially an infrared thermometer that you wield like a pistol, it's fairly simple to use. You point it around the room and it gives you the temperature. This helps you find "cold spots" and makes it easier to determine where cold air is entering the house. With this knowledge in hand, you can begin plugging those leaks. And once you start on a high-efficiency quest, you'll quickly learn that there are many places to look! From replacing your door thresholds and caulking the attic entrance to installing foam gaskets behind outlet and switch covers, there are many different ways to weatherproof the home. For more ideas, visit: http://energy.gov/ or try out the Home Energy Saver at http://hes.lbl.gov/consumer/.[1,2]

**Strange but True:** There are many other ways to insulate a house. In rural areas farmers have been known to stack extra hay bales around the outside of the house!

## Get Help from the Pros

Perhaps one of the best ways to improve your home's efficiency is to get an "energy audit" from a pro. While that may sound like a Scientology term, it's not. Many power companies offer Home Energy Audits.[1] They can range in price significantly (from walk-through audits that are $25 to more intensive audits that reach several hundred dollars). The premise remains the same: An expert in home efficiency will visit your home and help you identify areas where your house is energy inefficient and how to improve your residence's efficiency. If you don't have a house, energy audits also exist for apartments, although the types of changes you can make are obviously more limited. If you are more of a DIY-person, check out the Internet; there are many, many resources online; energy.gov is a great starting point.

# Winterizing Outside the House

There are a number of winterizing tasks to take care of outside the house as well. This list is by no means all-inclusive, but it's a good start.[1]

Before the snow flies, make sure your gutters are cleaned out. This is essential to prevent ice dams, which can cause quite a few problems. For more about ice dams, see page 79.

Caulk up any gaps on the exterior of the house/wall.

Make sure that dryer vents and other areas are free from debris.

If you live in a house with a garage, make sure you know how to manually open it. This way, if the power goes out, you can get your car out.

Disconnect hoses and put them away; on the interior of the house, turn off the actual water supply to the faucet (called the hose bibb); this prevents water from freezing in the faucet itself.[2]

Remove any dead trees that could possibly fall during a winter storm or tree limbs that could prove a problem.

If you set up holiday gear, do so ahead of time. It's a heck of a lot easier (and safer) to scale a ladder or string lights into your trees when there isn't ice and snow to contend with.[3]

Cover any other equipment in your yard (AC units, your boat and so on).

# What to Wear in Winter

Before you can leave the house, you need to know what to wear. The answer is actually pretty simple: layers of warm clothes. After all, it's what they do in Antarctica, where folks heading outdoors wear layers and layers of pretty high-end clothes.

Now we obviously don't need as many layers of gear as in Antarctica, but if you're planning on being outdoors for extended amounts of time, wearing layers is still effective for a few reasons. First, each layer of material helps you trap heat, which helps you stay toasty. Second, it's easy to adapt to temperature changes; if you get too warm, you can just remove one layer to adjust. Of course, you certainly don't need to dress up like a marshmallow at all times to survive a Minnesota winter, and layering isn't essential for every winter day. Often a thick coat will do the trick for your commute. Still, it's a handy tactic to keep in mind if you're constantly chilly or if you're working outdoors, ice fishing, snowmobiling or otherwise engaged in some serious winter adventuring.

# How to Layer

When layering, you should usually include three separate layers: a base layer, an insulating layer, and your outerwear. A simple pair of long johns simply isn't a good enough base layer for a winter camping trip. Thankfully, there are several different "weights" of gear; these include lightweight, mid-weight and "expedition" weight.[1] When in doubt, over-prepare. You can always stow away some more gear (my car's trunk is loaded with extras); it's always easier to throw on another layer than to shiver and wish you'd brought one along.

**IT COULD BE WORSE** Moisture control actually plagued early Arctic explorers. On Robert Falcon Scott's ill-fated *Terra Nova* expedition, the men man-hauled their sledges, causing them to sweat profusely despite the -40 temps. When they would set up camp, their clothing would retain the moisture and freeze. Things would get even worse after they entered their sleeping bags: As Apsley Cherry-Garrard noted in his book, *The Worst Journey in the World,* "Our sleeping-bags were awful. It took me . . . an hour of pushing and thumping and cramping every night to thaw out enough of mine to get into it at all. Even that was not so bad as lying in them when we got there."[1]

## Base Layer

When you're outdoors, you don't just have to worry about the cold; heat can actually be as troublesome. That is to say, working outdoors—even something as simple as tramping through snow—takes a good deal of effort, and this can cause you to sweat. If you sweat and you're wearing a material that absorbs moisture, that moisture will stick to your skin, and you'll find yourself getting cold, fast. That's why a good base layer is important; the right materials wick away moisture, helping you avoid the problem. Put simply, a base layer often consists of tight-fitting pants and a shirt made from Merino wool or polyesters. That everyday staple—cotton—isn't a great option, especially if it's quite cold and you'll be outdoors for a long period of time.

> **Note:** You can find cheap base layer options at department stores and the like, but be sure to choose clothing specifically designed for outdoor use; sporting-type shirts are cheap, but they don't perform as well.[1]

**Good Materials:**
- Polyester/polypropylene
- Wool

**Materials to Avoid:**
- 100 percent cotton (although some products have a mixture of cotton and synthetics)[2]

## Insulating Layer

As its name suggests, your insulating layer helps trap heat. If you're going outside for a short time, you can usually just wear a cotton sweater and get by fine (assuming you have proper outerwear). But if you're going outside for a length of time, you have to dress accordingly. A good wool sweater can be a bit bulky, but wool is both warm and durable. Fleece is another fine option, as is a goose down jacket, although goose down is ineffective if it gets wet. Goose down gets its insulating properties from its "loft," or the space between the feathery bits. When the feathers are wet, they collapse, and the insulation value is almost nonexistent. Thankfully, a new type of goose down—hydrophobic down—now exists.[1] It dries quickly and retains some insulating properties when wet, but it's spendy.

**Good Materials:**
- Wool
- Goose down (hydrophobic if you can afford it)
- Fleece

**Materials to Avoid:**
- 100 percent cotton
- Denim or khakis (as anyone who has shivered at a bus stop can attest, jeans are terrible insulators)

## Outer Layer

When it comes to winter gear, your outer layer is arguably the most important component of your winter wear. If your winter coat isn't windproof, waterproof, and warm, you're probably going to be cold no matter what. (Believe me: I love trench coats, but my thin trench coat is no match for December, let alone February.)

There are oodles of possible options, but be sure to get a winter coat that has down insulation. When it comes to insulation, down is still the best option (it's used in the jackets in Antarctica), although many coats now utilize a combination of synthetics and include down.

Whichever jacket you choose, you'll want pockets (preferably insulated ones) and a hood.

If you're out and about a lot, a full-fledged parka isn't a bad option, although they tend to be both expensive and bulky. If you're frequently outdoors, consider some coveralls or bibs; often sold at Fleet Farm and the like, these outfits are popular among tow truck drivers, folks ice fishing, and others.

**Good Materials:**
- Goose down

**Materials to Avoid:**
- 100 percent cotton
- Denim

## Explaining Jacket Fill Amounts

Buying a jacket can be a bit perplexing, thanks to a bit of jargon that's involved: a jacket's "fill power." Fill power is essentially a measurement of the quality of the down used in the jacket. Fill power is actually a measurement of volume; it's the amount of room an ounce of a given type of down takes up when it's compressed. So one ounce of 800 fill down will take up 800 cubic inches when compressed; 700 down will only take up 700. Down gets its insulating properties from

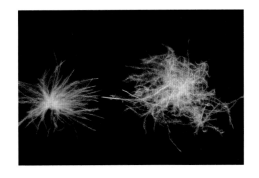

its volume, which is known as its "loft."[1] Essentially, all the space between feathers traps heat, so the higher the number, the better the down (and the more expensive it is). What's more, jackets with higher fill volumes are often lighter/less bulky, as it takes less down to insulate the coat. Generally, jackets with 600 power fill down are a good compromise between warmth and price, as products with the highest fill ratings can get quite expensive.

**What Is Down, Exactly, and Where Does It Come from?** It might be surprising, but doesn't actually consist of traditional feathers. As anyone with a feather pillow knows, the exterior feathers on a bird are fairly large, firm and have a long quill at the end. Down, on the other hand, essentially consists of a very soft "fluff" without the traditional feather's firm quill. Down is usually found beneath a bird's primary feathers, although many baby birds are born only with a coating of down. The down in jackets usually comes from ducks (such as the famous Eider species) or from geese. In most cases, the feathers are usually a by-product of the poultry industry and are not plucked from the birds.

**Strange but True:** On his ill-fated attempt to reach the South Pole in 1911, Robert Falcon Scott's expedition wore clothes provided by the famous clothing company Burberry, which is today known for its very high-end trench coats and the like.

# Covering up the Rest of You

If you've got your layers figured out, it's time to cover your hands, feet, neck, and head. The human body loses a lot of heat from the face, neck and head, so you need to cover those areas, especially if the temperatures drop and the wind is up.

## Hats

Above all, make sure your hat choice is thick enough to be warm, windproof and water-resistant. In my experience, the cheap cotton hats you can pick up for a buck or two at department stores aren't very warm or weather resistant. I love warm bomber hats, trapper's hats, and Stormy Kromer hats, because they help keep your ears covered and because they often have clips that snap around your chin. Sure, you look like Elmer Fudd, but you stay a lot warmer. There are many options that don't scream "I'm hunting wabbits," however; many snowboarding companies offer beanies that are quite warm, and your average outdoors-themed store will carry a variety of options. Whichever hat you choose, get one that is lined, as this added layer of insulation really comes in handy.

The materials found in hats are often pretty similar to those in your insulation layers: wool, polyester and such, although they often include a water-resistant coating.

When it gets really cold and you have to be outside, consider a ski mask (also known as a balaclava.) Sure, you'll look like you're about to rob a bank, but they are one of the best ways to keep your whole face from freezing.

### What Not to Wear

- Your average baseball caps will not do the trick. They are usually uninsulated and leave your ears unprotected.

- Avoid cheap stocking caps; they don't tend to be all that warm, and the wind often goes right through them.

---

**Strange but True:** The balaclava gets its name from the battle of the same name in the Crimean War; that battle is perhaps most famous for inspiring Tennyson's famous poem "The Charge of the Light Brigade."[1]

## Shoes, Boots and Socks

Let's talk socks first. When it gets really cold, cotton socks are next to worthless. They don't insulate very well and they retain moisture (which can affect how well your boots/shoes insulate).[1] So be sure to pick up some real winter socks. Wool is an ever-popular option, but synthetic options exist as well. Such socks usually come in single pairs (or packs of three) and are often fairly expensive, but when you pick up a pair, you'll see why; they're heavy and wonderfully warm.

When it comes to shoes/boots, you're going to want something with some traction (for walking on ice); many hiking-style shoes and work boots are designed with traction in mind. You'll also need insulation for when it gets really cold (or when there is a big snowstorm). In my opinion, any Minnesota resident needs at least one pair of serious winter boots. These can be expensive, but they are worth it. Work boots are a good option, as they are often rated by temperature and made for use outdoors. With a little effort, you can even find such boots for every member of the family. (Outdoors-themed stores are often a good place to look.)

### What Not to Wear
- Thin shoes. Tennis shoes and sneakers are made for warmer climes than ours. The same goes for many types of women's shoes and even "fashion" boots. If you're stuck out in the cold for any length of time, you're going to want dedicated winter gear.

## Gloves

You've also got to keep your hands warm. Finding a good pair of gloves is tough. Warmer gloves tend to be fairly bulky, making it hard to actually do anything with your hands while wearing them; this is especially true if you want to use a touch screen on a smartphone. Mittens can be warm, but it's hard to do anything while wearing them, as your hands are essentially reduced to lobster claws.

Some thin gloves exist and claim to make it possible to use your cell phone, but this takes some getting used to, and it's certainly not foolproof. (If you have bulky gloves, you can always use a stylus and keep your gloves on.) Still, they are usually warm enough for your average commute, but you'll want a warmer pair socked away if you're stuck outdoors. Keeping a pair of heavy-duty ice fishing gloves in your car is a good idea, especially if you need to change a flat tire in February. (I've been there, and believe me, if you have to take your gloves off to actually grasp a tire iron or a lug nut, you'll get cold in a hurry.)

### What Not To Wear
- Thin cotton gloves cost $2 for a reason; they are better than nothing, but not by much.

## Dressing for Winter Exercise

Layering is important to stay warm, but dressing too warmly can be its own problem if you're exerting a great deal of effort when working outdoors.[1] Finding the right balance for your activity (say, running or fat-tire biking) can take some trial-and-error, but it's well worth it; maintaining an active outdoors lifestyle is a great way to avoid cabin fever.

## Keep Your Kids in Mind and Don't Forget Your Furry Friends

If you've got little ones, be sure that you bundle them up. Children lose heat faster than adults, so you need to make sure they are wearing enough warm gear. In addition, don't forget your pets: Dogs and cats are affected by wind chill just like people, and a dog's paws are often very sensitive and susceptible to freezing. What's more, dogs are susceptible to low humidity and often sensitive to the chemicals in some ice melts; ask your veterinarian for recommendations.[1]

**A Public Service Announcement:** Inevitably, you will see insane people wearing shorts, even on the coldest days of a Minnesota winter. Please, do not be one of those people.

**IT COULD BE WORSE** The Jack London short story "To Build a Fire" revolves around a cold snap in the Yukon where it reaches -60 degrees. The good news? It's only gotten that cold here in Minnesota on one occasion. Still, the moral of the story stands: be prepared.

# Cold Weather Ailments

## Frostbite

Human skin consists of three primary layers: the epidermis (the outer layer of the skin), the dermis (a layer that helps support the skin structurally) and the subcutis, which helps connect the dermis to the tissue below and also stores fat.[1] As in the rest of the human body, water is essential to skin function, but if you don't dress warmly enough, you put yourself at risk of frostbite, which occurs when human skin begins to freeze at a cellular level.[2] Just as the severity of burns is evaluated in terms of "degrees" there are several different stages of frostbite, each with its own "degree" of severity.[3] Generally speaking, the deeper the skin freezes, the more damage it causes. The three main types of frostbite are as follows:

### Frostnip

The first phase of frostbite is known as frostnip. The primary symptoms are a general feeling of cold, followed by "pinpricks" and numbness.[1] The affected skin turns pale or red. Once the skin is rewarmed, it becomes tender and may hurt. Thankfully, frostnip doesn't cause any permanent damage, but get it checked out by a doctor if you're not sure.[2]

### Superficial Frostbite

If frostbite progresses past frostnip, superficial frostbite begins to develop. The skin that had turned pale or red will become white or gray. Bizarrely, the skin may itself feel warm, but according to the Mayo Clinic, that's a sign of serious trouble.[1] Once you warm that skin up again, you'll likely feel pain or a stinging sensation, possibly followed by formation of a blister. Superficial frostbite usually doesn't cause permanent damage, but in some cases it can lead to complications. When in doubt, see a doctor![2]

## Severe/Deep Frostbite

The most serious type of frostbite, severe frostbite could be thought of as "deep" frostbite. Ice crystals form not just on the surface of the skin but deeper within it (and eventually even in skin cells themselves). When water freezes, it expands, and this eventually does a great deal of damage to the cells and the surrounding area. This creates a cascade effect that eventually leads to tissue death.[1] The result is not a pretty sight: Severely frostbitten skin is entirely numb, and it eventually blisters, the tissue beneath hardening to a black, green or yellow. Take my advice: Never do a Google image search for this.[2] As any-

one familiar with the history of polar exploration or mountaineering is aware, in cases of severe frostbite, amputations are often the last resort. Needless to say, if you suspect you have severe frostbite, get medical help immediately.

**IT COULD BE WORSE** Frostbite has a long (and awful) history in war. Hannibal, the famous general from Carthage, led an entire army, including war elephants(!) across the Alps mountain range; along the way, he lost about half of his army, many to the cold.[1] By the time he actually invaded Italy, he didn't have all that many troops left to fight the Romans. The armies of Napoleon Bonaparte and Adolf Hitler suffered terribly from frostbite and cold as well, as both leaders opted to fight a war that persisted into a severe Russian winter. The Nazis assumed a quick victory, so they brought only light summer gear, and frostbite and hypothermia devastated them. The Eastern Front Medal was eventually issued to participants from the German Wehrmacht (Army), and they quickly dubbed it the *Gefrierfleischorden*, or "Badge of the Frozen Flesh."[2]

## How Long Does It Take to Get Frostbite?

According to the Mayo Clinic, once the temps drop into the single digits (usually below 5 degrees), the risk of frostbite rises.[1] The length of time needed for frostbite to occur depends on a number of factors, including wind speed, temperature, exposure time, humidity and medical conditions/factors. In exceptionally cold/windy weather, it can happen very quickly, within 10 or even 5 minutes of exposure. Worse yet, once initial frostbite (and the resulting numbness) sets in, it can be hard to realize you've been affected. See the wind chill exposure chart on page 26 for a rough timeline.

## Frostbite Treatment

If you think you have frostbite, seek medical care. If you can't get care right away, be sure to get indoors as soon as you can.[1] But there's a catch: walking on frostbitten feet can make the damage worse, so avoid using the frostbitten areas as much as possible. Once indoors, warm the frostbitten areas. You can do so by using body heat or by using warm (but not hot!) water. According to the Centers for Disease Control, the water should be comfortable to the touch for areas of your body that weren't frostbitten.[2] Once you're able, get to a doctor for a professional evaluation.

### How Not to Treat Frostbite

Don't rub frostbitten areas or massage them. Rubbing frostbite with snow was once considered the proper procedure; this actually can cause additional damage.[1]

Also, don't use a heating pad, a stove, an open fire or a radiator to warm up. Frostbite causes numbness, making it quite likely that you'll inadvertently burn your already damaged skin.

**How to Avoid Frostbite:** Pay attention to the weather forecast; a portable weather radio is never a bad idea. (Many of the battery-powered models also have hand-crank options and plug-ins for cell phone chargers.)

- Dress warmly and limit time spent outdoors if temperatures are low and wind speeds are high.

- Keep a charged cell phone and a set of car keys handy ,so you can call in the cavalry if necessary. Just in case, keep extra gear in your car or somewhere else can access should the weather turn cold.

- Monitor the young and the elderly, as they are more susceptible to frostbite.

- Be mindful about consuming alcohol in the cold; drinking alcohol gives one the immediate sensation of warmth, but it's something of a mirage; frostbite actually occurs more quickly if someone is under the influence of alcohol.[1]

### The Science of Frostbite

Frostbite is actually a chain reaction of sorts. When extremities (the most likely areas to become frostbitten) are exposed to cold, the body often reacts with the Hunting Response, which is named for a phenomenon first noticed in hunters who were accustomed to the winter cold.[1] When exposed to cold, the hunters' bodies reacted by increasing blood flow to the area, then constricting it. This temporarily warms the area, but is followed by a steep temperature

drop. If exposure continues, this process repeats, and as it does, the skin temperature drops. Eventually, the skin becomes cold enough to freeze; if exposure continues, this accelerates the process, causing damage to deepen. Even if a person finds a warm shelter, the damage isn't necessarily finished. Frostbite isn't just a problem of freezing. Repeated thawing and freezing can do additional damage.[2] Long story short, if you suspect frostbite, get to a medical professional ASAP.[3]

# Hypothermia

Frostbite isn't the only winter weather worry to keep in mind. Hypothermia is another real threat, and it can even occur when the weather is above freezing. The human body has an average temperature of around 98.6 degrees; hypothermia occurs when the body's core temperature (around the internal organs) drops to 95 degrees or lower.[1] Once that threshold is reached, brain function and coordination decreases, making an already dangerous situation worse, as hypothermia makes it more difficult (and sometimes impossible) for victims to rescue themselves.[2] This double-whammy is what makes any case of hypothermia a medical emergency.

Hypothermia can occur by sudden exposure to cold water (such as falling into a cold lake or falling through lake or river ice), but it can also occur when folks are improperly dressed and are exposed to cold weather for a long period of time.[3] In some cases, hypothermia can even occur indoors in poorly heated buildings (or in those without heat altogether).[4]

Minnesota's 10,000 Lakes and (our innumerable streams and rivers) are the source of most hypothermia deaths in the state, as most deaths occur when snowmobilers, anglers or outdoor enthusiasts inadvertently fall through the ice and are submerged in freezing water.[5] According to the DNR, over the past thirty years, about 6 people have died each year from falling into cold water (or breaking through ice), although that total has been decreasing in the past few decades.[6]

## Hypothermia Symptoms[1]

According to the Mayo Clinic, the early phases of hypothermia (body temperature of 95-90 degrees) are marked by a number of symptoms, including shivering, dizziness, nausea, hunger, confusion, difficulty speaking, coordination issues and fatigue.[2,3]

In more severe cases of hypothermia—usually somewhere around 90 degrees and lower—symptoms are more pronounced and include clumsiness, slurred speech and poor decision-making.[4] Respiration and heart rate also slow.

If a patient isn't rewarmed, temps continue to drop and shivering actually stops. Eventually, the patient may become unconscious and experience cardiac arrest or hypovolemic shock (fluid loss that makes it difficult for the heart to pump blood effectively through the body).[5]

## Hypothermia Treatment[1]

- If you suspect hypothermia, call 911 and seek medical care immediately; this is serious stuff.

- If possible, get the person inside to a warm place; if you can't, try to shelter them and keep them off the cold ground.

- If they have wet clothing on, get them out of it and give them dry clothes or blankets.

- Start by rewarming their abdomen, head, neck and core region; heat wraps or an electric blanket work; don't worry about the arms/legs at first.[2]

- Give them a warm, sweet drink but no alcohol, which makes the body lose heat more quickly; have the victim abstain from cigarettes as well.[3]

- Don't rewarm the person too quickly (as in a hot tub or a hot bath); in addition, don't massage their limbs.

- If the person isn't breathing, perform CPR; in some cases, a hypothermic person may appear "dead" but can be revived; (see below for more on that).

## Hypothermic Responses

### Brought Back from the Brink

There's a saying in medicine: You're not dead until you're warm and dead. As it turns out, hypothermia isn't always a death sentence. Even though severe hypothermia often kills, some people with severe hypothermia can be resuscitated, and some even survive with no neurological damage.[1] Amazingly, resuscitation can sometimes occur after a significant amount of time has passed. In one case, a boy broke through a frozen lake and drowned. He was resuscitated after 88 minutes and made a full recovery. In another case, a patient survived after 6 hours of resuscitation.[2,3] The success rate isn't high, however; only a fraction of patients survive, and many have some degree of neurological deficit afterward.

---

**Strange but True:** When a hypothermic patient is rewarmed, sometimes they start improving, only to experience "rewarming shock." If untreated, this can cause a recovering patient to suddenly die. Thankfully, doctors are generally aware of the problem and can take steps to prevent it.[1,2]

### The Diving Reflex

So how do some hypothermic patients survive? After all, they aren't breathing and their heart stops. They should be dead, right? Not exactly. They likely survive due to a quirk of mammalian evolution called the Diving Reflex. When a mammal's face makes contact with cold water, its heart rate lowers and blood is redistributed to the body's core.[1] This slows the metabolism, reducing the need for oxygen consumption, effectively delaying damage to the brain. As humans are mammals, we possess this reflex, and it's likely what enables rescuers to attempt resuscitation on people who appear to be dead. (The Diving Reflex is quite strong in children, and they have a higher survival rate than adults in hypothermia cases.) What's more, in case of cardiac arrest, doctors now sometimes actually induce mild hypothermia in patients who aren't hypothermic, as hypothermia sometimes confers a mild survival advantage for those undergoing cardiac arrest.[2,3]

## Paradoxical Undressing

When a person becomes hypothermic, their body shunts blood from the extremities to the core. Eventually, the body loses the ability to continue doing so, and blood surges back to the long-cold extremities. It's thought that this pronounced temperature differential leads the person to feel as if they are burning up (when they really are at the tail end of freezing to death). In response, severely hypothermic people often tear off their clothes in an attempt to cool down, dying soon thereafter.[1]

## Terminal Burrowing

When victims who die of exposure are found, they are often found "burrowed" or hidden beneath an item or another object. Like the Diving Reflex, this behavior is thought to be a reflex shared by all mammals, including humans. Essentially, it's a last-ditch attempt to seek shelter, in much the same way that hibernating animals dig to escape the cold.[1] Sometimes, hypothermia victims exhibit both Paradoxical Undressing and Terminal Burrowing, giving an already macabre scene and even more bizarre feel.

# Other Cold-Weather Ailments

## Trench Foot

If your feet are exposed to cold, wet conditions for an extended length of time, you can develop Trench Foot (also known as immersion foot).[1] Over time, the feet become cold and numb, and once they are warmed back up, they begin to hurt. If left unchecked, Trench Foot can lead to tissue and muscle death. The best way to prevent it is to keep your feet dry and warm, to avoid tight-fitting boots, to change socks often and to inspect the feet regularly for signs of damage.[2] Trench Foot gets its name from World War I, where it ravaged armies on all sides, leading to 75,000 casualties among the Allies alone.[3]

## Chilblains

While chilblains may sound like some sort of Victorian-era curse, it's a real malady.[1] Often confused with trench foot, chilblains is an inflammatory condition that occurs due to an abnormal response to cold exposure. It leads to red or bluish, painful toes and is often a symptom of other diseases.[2]

## Sunburn

Given that your average December day only has eight or nine hours of sunlight, you might think that sunburns are out of the question. This isn't actually true. If you're out and about for an extended length of time, you can get a sunburn, even in winter.[1] So you'll need to wear sunscreen on any exposed areas. In addition, you'll also want to wear lip balm that contains sunscreen; this will protect you from the dreaded chapped lips and help you avoid sunburned lips, which are as painful as they sound.

# Digging Out

Fall is a lovely season in Minnesota, but it has a bitter ending. As late October turns to November, it starts to get cold, and the skies are often overcast. All of this—like the season itself—is a portent of the winter to come. As much as you try to will it away— and all Minnesota residents will try this at some point—it'll never work. The first storm hits eventually. You go to bed with the lawn still mostly green, and a few holdout trees still with leaves. You wake up and you find yourself inside a snow globe. And then you have to dig out. To do so, you need to know what gear you'll need, and once you can actually escape your driveway, you'll need to know how to get around.

# Snow Removal Gear

Before you can shovel your driveway or clean up the walk, you need the right gear. From snow-plows attached to vehicles to electric snow shovels, there are a number of different options for snow removal, but if you drive around your average neighborhood, you'll find that most people opt for snowblowers or the humble snow shovel.

## Snow Shovels

Let's start with the snow shovel. For a relatively simple tool, there are many different varieties of shovels. Some are made with ergonomics in mind, whereas others are cheap, mass-produced and about as simple as they come.

### Shovel Recommendations

Be wary of plastic shovels. Plastic shovels are just fine for light, powdery snow, but when you inevitably get decked by a storm with wet, heavy snow, your plastic shovels won't be up to the task. (Take it from me, I once broke two plastic shovels in the same storm.) Instead, be sure to have at least one heavy-duty shovel with a wide steel blade and a sturdy wooden handle. These are more expensive and can be heavy, but they shouldn't fall apart on you.

Have more than one shovel; this is important for a few reasons. First, you'll need one if a shovel breaks. Second, it's handy to have several shovels. That way, your spouse/significant other/children/neighbors can help, if they're willing.

Also, have two different types of shovels on hand. The wide, heavy steel shovels are great for clearing big mounds of snow (but you often have to put your body weight against it if the snow is heavy). The smaller, thinner shovels are good for cleaning up leftover snow.

## Shoveling Tips

First and foremost, buy your snow removal gear before the first storm hits! When a storm hits, everyone and their sister will be buying gear, and it often sells out.

- Shoveling is pretty self-explanatory; obviously you need to dress warmly. But once you're there, most folks just divide the driveway/walkway into "rows" and clear off one row at a time. If there is a lot of snow, you'll need to make additional passes for each row (as the excess snow will be pushed to the side).

- Also, if the storm is forecast to drop a lot of snow, you're going to want to start shoveling before all the snow has hit; this way, you can keep the shoveling more manageable. This means that you have to shovel twice (or even three times), but believe me, it's a lot easier to clear off four inches of snow on two separate occasions than struggling to shovel eight inches of wet snow.

- Do not shovel snow into the road; this is illegal.

- If you've shoveled your driveway, keep in mind that you'll likely have to shovel the bottom of your driveway again once a plow has come by. If the storm has dropped a lot of snow, this can require quite a bit of work.

- If you live in a cul-de-sac, a plow may pile up snow in your yard. These piles can get pretty large (and can even damage low-hanging branches, so keep your trees trimmed).

- In many areas, it's your responsibility to shovel sidewalks and get rid of ice; some cities take care of this for their residents, but they are the exception rather than the rule. If you don't shovel your sidewalk, you can be ticketed, or even held liable should an injury occur.

- Don't over-exert yourself when shoveling; in a certain subset of the population (folks with existing cardiovascular trouble and a sedentary lifestyle), shoveling may even trigger heart attacks.[1]

- Don't forget about your furry friends; be sure to shovel your walkway and clear off an area in the grass (if you have a yard).

## Snowblower Selection

All snowblowers use augurs to propel snow out of a manually adjusted chute, but there are two primary types of snowblowers: those with two stages and those with one stage. One-stage snowblowers have a relatively simple setup. The engine runs the augur, which contacts the ground and sends the snow through the chute. One-stage snowblowers usually aren't self-propelled, which means you have to push them. A two-phase snowblower has an added component (called an impeller) that accelerates the snow and throws it farther. This type of snowblower also features motorized wheels, helping to move the machine and preventing the augur blades from touching the ground.[1]

So which one should you choose? Here are the pros and cons.

### Benefits of a One-Stage Snowblower

- simpler, and therefore cheaper

- smaller and more compact

- runs on either gas or electric power

- doesn't require as much maintenance

### Drawbacks of a One-Stage Snowblower

- not self-propelled

- augur contacts the ground, not suited for gravel or rock driveways

- narrower, more passes needed

- struggles with heavy, wet snow or large amounts of snow

- electric models need to be plugged in

## Benefits of a Two-Stage Snowblower

- designed for heavy-duty work

- wider, handles more snow in each pass

- ideal for handling all varieties of snow

- self-propelled

- no extension cords necessary

## Drawbacks of a Two-Stage Snowblower

- more expensive (often several hundred dollars)

- bigger and takes up a lot of room

- needs regular maintenance

## Snowblower Safety

Snowblowers are potentially dangerous, and if used improperly or carelessly, they can cause injuries.[1] Most injuries are caused when the chute clogs with snow and users attempt to reach inside it with their hands to clear the snow out. This is very dangerous, even if the machine is off. That's worth repeating: **You can be seriously injured by a clogged snowblower even if it's off**.[2] How, you ask? Well, as it turns out, a University of Arkansas study determined that when snow becomes clogged in a chute, it retains some of the rotational force, and when you free the snow, that force causes the blades to rotate about one full turn, more than enough to hurt you. So the moral of the story is **never use your hand to clear out a clogged chute**. Instead, read your owner's manual for its recommendations; many snowblowers now come with purpose-made tools to remove clogs. (If yours didn't, you can order them online.)

## What about Electric Shovels?

Electric shovels are something of a hybrid option—essentially motorized shovels. They are electrically powered (and need an extension cord). They tend to be fairly narrow and tend to struggle with even relatively moderate amounts of snow. With that said, they are fairly inexpensive ($90) and can make it easier to clear a walkway or even help clean up a driveway. They too can become clogged, so be sure to use them with care and read your owner's manual.

## Other Accessories

You might want to have an ice chopper handy. These consist of a small, steel blade on a wooden handle and look a bit like a medieval weapon of some kind. As their name suggests, they are very useful for chopping up thick ice (or sliding beneath it to loosen it).

## Snow Removal Services

If you're unable to shovel or just plain hate it, you can contact a snow removal service. Many snow removal services exist, and they vary from neighborhood kids willing to do the shoveling for you up to full-fledged commercial operations. Rates vary, obviously, and it's always good to have your service scheduled ahead of a storm.

# Ice Buildup
## Sidewalk

Once the snow is cleaned up, you still have to worry about ice. One of the best ways to prevent ice formation is via sidewalk salt (which is usually sold in the form of rock salt). The premise is the same as the road salt you'll see plows spreading: Salt lowers the freezing point of water, making it harder for ice to build up. Of course, if the temp drops too low, salt becomes ineffective. (That's why it's handy to also spread some sand on especially icy areas, as it helps to provide some traction.)

> **Note:** Rock salt can be hazardous for pets (as it can harm their paws and cause gastro-intestinal issues).[1] If you've got a furry friend, ask your veterinarian about which pet-safe version they recommend. Also, be prepared to open your wallet; sidewalk salt tends to be somewhat spendy.

## Ice Dams

If you've never heard of one, you might think that an ice dam is the wintertime work of an exceptionally industrious beaver. Sadly, it's not; instead, it's a major hassle for homeowners. Ice

dams form when heat rises to the roof of a house, and escapes, eventually melting snow, which freezes on the house's eaves. This ice builds up in a "dam," and some of the ice beneath melts and can find its way into the house, wrecking insulation and leading to mold growth. The ice buildup on the outside can cause damage to the roof and shingles or pose a danger to those directly below the ice dam.

## Ice Dam Prevention

To prevent ice dams, you either need to prevent heat from escaping or ensure that the entire roof remains the same temperature. You can do this either by adding insulation (to the attic, ductwork and other areas where heat escapes) or ensuring that your roof is well ventilated. (A well-ventilated roof will stay the same temperature—cold!—preventing the snow from melting to begin with.) Also be sure to keep your gutters clean, as clogged gutters serve as a base for ice formation.

## Signs of an Ice Dam

Of course, knowing how to prevent an ice dam isn't particularly helpful once you have one. Telltale signs of an ice dam include water seepage in ceilings/walls in the top level of your home; also keep an eye on the icicles on your house.[1] If there seems to be water behind the icicles, it's probably time to get it checked out.

## Removing an Ice Dam

If you suspect an ice dam and you know water is entering your house, the first thing to do is call a professional. (It can lead to mold growth and such, water damage is serious business.) If you don't think water is entering the structure, there are ways to attempt to address ice dams yourself, but the following are short-term fixes, and don't address the long-term problem.

- Put a fan in the attic or near where the water is coming in; this will lower the temperature and cause any melting water to freeze, preventing water from entering the structure.[1]

- Because ice dams form when snow melts, you can halt ice dam formation by removing the snow with a snow rake. These special tools have very long handles that enable you to remove the roof's snow while standing at ground level. If possible, opt for a snow rake with wheels, as it prevents roof damage.[2] Obviously, be careful when removing snow in this manner, as it's not hard to dislodge the ice dam itself or inadvertently bury yourself (in very heavy) snow. You also need to avoid power lines and the like.

- You can attempt to melt a "trough" in the ice dam by filling a pantyhose leg with calcium chloride (not rock salt, which can damage your house and kill your plants below). This will create a channel that melts the ice. But you need to place the sock vertically on the ice dam. Be very careful when placing such a device, however, as it's easy to slip and fall when placing one.[3]

## What Not to Do

- Don't hack at the ice dam with a shovel or an ice chopper; these tools usually only have short handles and you'll be standing directly beneath anything you dislodge. This may also damage your house.

- Avoid going up on the roof, if at all possible. Working on the roof is dangerous enough as it is in the summer; in the winter, it's strictly for professionals.

***IT COULD BE WORSE*** Be careful around ice dams and icicles. Deaths due to "roof avalanches" and falling ice aren't unheard of. And that icicle hanging from the roof of the building you're walking under? If a ten-pound icicle falls from 40 feet and hits you square in the head, it'll produce over 1,300 pounds of force.[1] For frame of reference, Frank Bruno, a former heavyweight champion of the world punched with about the same force. And things only get worse if the icicles get bigger or fall from higher up.[2]

## How Much Snow Is Too Much for the Roof to Handle?

If it's a really snowy winter, you may start to worry about your roof. Buildings with flat (or narrowly peaked roofs) are most at risk, but if a roof has suffered structural damage or alteration, it could be at risk as well. Generally speaking, most structurally sound homes should be OK, but under extreme conditions, the weight of all that snow can begin to cause damage.[1] One way to diagnose this is by checking the doors in your house. If some of them suddenly begin to stick or jam, then there might be undue pressure on the house.[2] The same goes for obvious structural problems.

Whatever you do, don't try to remove snow by going up on the roof yourself. Roof snow removal is tricky (and dangerous) business and is best handled by the pros. When in doubt, call in the cavalry.

## Shoveling the Deck

If you have a deck, you might wonder if you need to shovel it. Generally speaking, if your deck doesn't have any other problems and was designed correctly, your deck doesn't need to be shoveled until the snow is above the railings.[1] If you decide to shovel your deck, be sure to use a plastic (not metal!) shovel and go with the grain (not against it), as it's really, really easy to gouge the deck or remove the deck's stain. Also, don't use rock salt, as it's essentially guaranteed to wreck the finish on your deck.

# (Trying to) Leave the House

When a few inches of snow hits down south, life grinds to a halt. But not in Minnesota. We dig out, scrape the snow and ice off the car, and life goes on. (After all, those groceries aren't going to buy themselves.) But if you haven't lived through a Minnesota winter, somebody has to show you the ropes; heck, even if you're a longtime resident, the following information about driving, shoveling and, yes, even biking during winter in the Land of 10,000 (frozen) Lakes may prove useful.

# How to Walk in Winter: Embrace Your Inner Penguin

Penguins may live in Antarctica, but they can teach folks in the North Country a lot about how to avoid falls. Shuffling or waddling is one of the best ways to avoid falls; while it's not fool-proof, it helps you keep your balance, and if you do fall, you'll be moving more slowly and more likely to fall on your rear end.[1,2] Also, keep your hands out of your pockets, and if at all possible stick to areas with handrails or other supports.

If you walk outdoors a lot or are especially worried about falling, ice cleats are an option. These metal crampon or chain-like devices are similar to those worn by ice climbers, and they surround your footwear, helping you keep a steady grip. They are a bit unwieldy, however, and you need to remove them before venturing indoors or driving.

## If You Fall

If you fall, don't try to catch yourself with your arms; this is an easy way to break a bone. Instead, close up in a ball as you fall and try to land on your rear end, if possible.

If you experience a fall, see a doctor; this is especially true if you're older or on medication, as some medications can turn a normal "fall" into a medical emergency.

**Sad but True:** According to the CDC, from 1999 to 2013 a whopping 1,412 people died because of a fall due to ice and snow; that total includes 88 Minnesotans.[1] Not surprisingly, no deaths due to falls from ice or snow were reported in Florida. Most, but not all, of the deaths were among those aged 55 and older.

# Driving in Winter or How to Leave the House
## Winterize Your Car

Before winter hits, you need to winterize your car. Winter driving is tough on a vehicle, and a breakdown in winter isn't just annoying; it can be dangerous if the temperatures drop low enough. That's why it's helpful to bring your car into a shop that you trust before the snow flies. The following list isn't all-inclusive—when in doubt, consult a trusted mechanic—but these areas of your car are especially important to check out.

### Your Car's Battery

Winter is bad enough for everyone, but it's especially hard on your battery. Many battery problems begin in summer, however. Hot, humid weather leads to increased corrosion—and uses the battery's internal reserves more quickly. These problems are most likely to show up when it's cold, though, as it requires more juice to start a car in cold weather than in warm weather and because cold weather causes a battery's power capacity to drop precipitously.[1,2] (The colder it gets, the worse things are on your battery.)

Thankfully, there are steps to ensure your vehicle starts up. First things first, have your battery checked out—batteries get weaker as they age and eventually need replacement, usually after four years or so. In addition, have an auto tech clean off any corrosion (which can build up

during the summer) on the battery terminals, cables and such. Also consider buying a battery charger; charging your battery can help maintain its lifespan, but read your owner's manual thoroughly or consult with an expert before charging a battery.[3] Doing so incorrectly can be dangerous.

## General Maintenance[1]

Oil is akin to the lifeblood of an engine, so getting an oil change and performing other routine maintenance is important, especially if winter's coming.[2] Read your car's owner's manual, and be sure to follow all the recommended maintenance—they don't put it in there for nothing. If you know a trusty mechanic, it's helpful to visit them in the fall and have them do all the work for you at once.

## Windshield Wipers

It may sound simple, but you want good windshield wipers before the snow hits. Replacing them is easy, even for complete novices. And as far as auto repairs go, it's relatively cheap. (Specially designed winter blades are available as well.[1]) You'll also need to stock up on windshield washer fluid that won't freeze, so be sure to read the labels carefully when purchasing some. (Summer mixes are only rated to temperatures around freezing, so you need to switch to the cold-weather stuff.)

Also, don't use your windshield fluid to get rid of ice. This works, but it's an easy way to damage the rubber on your windshield wipers.[2]

## Brakes and Tires

You need to go into winter with your brakes in good condition, as you'll definitely be needing them. Tire condition is essential, too. It might be surprising, but not all tires are created equally. Some tires—such as low profile tires—aren't well suited for our winter weather. As their name implies, all-weather tires are a popular option in Minnesota, but some drivers opt for special snow tires. (In areas with significant elevation changes, including the Pacific Northwest, tire chains are popular.)

You don't just need the right kind of tires; they also have to be in good condition. Worn tires are especially dangerous, so it's essential that you have the condition of your tires checked by a pro. Also, make sure your tires are properly inflated to the manufacturer's specifications, and check your tire pressure periodically during the winter, as cold temperatures cause pressure tire to drop. Because flats are common in the winter, double-check that your spare is in good shape and your tire jack and your tire iron are easily accessible.

For a good run-down of tire safety (and how to check tire tread and pressure yourself), see the U.S. Department of Transportation's Tire Safety page: www.nhtsa.gov/Vehicle+Safety/Tires

### Have the Coolant System Checked

In the summer, a car's coolant system helps prevent the vehicle from overheating; in the winter, the same system helps prevent a car from freezing, preventing major damage to the engine. That's why you need to make sure your vehicle's antifreeze level is sufficient and the mix is correct. Check your owner's manual for info about your vehicle. You'll also want to make sure that the rest of the coolant/heating system is in working order. If you suspect a problem or a leak, get it fixed in fall rather than in winter.

### Defroster and Heat

These two are obvious. If you don't have heat, you'll know it, and you'll be miserable (and quite possibly frostbitten). Perhaps worse yet, if your car isn't producing heat, your defroster won't work, and you're in trouble in a hurry.[1] So if you notice problems with your heat on those cold November mornings, get it checked out ASAP.

### Exhaust

Carbon monoxide poisoning can be a problem in cars, too, and this is especially true in winter, when we run our cars a lot more than in the summer. So you need to make sure your exhaust system is in good shape. If you suspect a leak of some variety, get it fixed, as you'll be running your car a lot in the winter.

### Gas It Up

Keep your gas tank full in winter; while gasoline resists freezing, it sometimes contains water, and this can freeze in the fuel lines, making it difficult for your car to start. Having a full tank makes this less likely to occur. Also, there are several types of products you can add (ISO-HEET is one of them) that prevent ice formation, making it less likely your fuel lines will freeze.[1]

## Car Kit

Once your car is shipshape (carshape?), gassed up and ready for winter, it's helpful to assemble a car kit. If you've never lived in Minnesota, the idea of an emergency kit for winter might seem strange, but it's always a good idea to have one on hand, just in case.

If all goes well, you'll never need some of the items in this kit, but if you do, you'll be happy.

- An ice scraper with a snow brush: the scraper helps you remove ice buildup on your windows and windshield, and the snow brush helps you unbury your car.

- A cell phone and a cell phone charger. Ideally, you'll have two chargers: one that uses your car's cigarette adapter, and one that attaches to an emergency weather radio. These often have manually powered cranks, giving you a failsafe option. Hopefully, these are the only parts of your emergency kit you'll never need to use.

- Blankets/hand warmers/extra cold-weather gear: In our busy, working world, we forget stuff, but if you misplace a glove or your hat and find yourself stranded, you'll regret it. That's why it's handy to keep an extra set of cold-weather gear in your trunk.

- First Aid Kits are essential any time of year, so make sure to keep your kit stocked and ready.

- Jumper cables help transfer energy from a running car's battery to a dead battery; before attempting to jump your car (or someone else's) be sure you know what you're doing; for instructions and safety considerations, see page 103.

- A travel shovel: You read that right. Travel shovels are a real thing, and they will undoubtedly come in handy when you inadvertently bury your car in a snowbank; I've used mine dozens of times (both to unbury my car and to help others out).

- Kitty litter and a few thin wooden boards (say, three feet long or so): While these items don't sound like much, they are great tools to help you get your car unstuck; the kitty litter and sand help your tires get more traction, and the wooden boards both help your wheels get traction and cover any icy gouges your spinning wheels may have made; cardboard can even work in a pinch.

- A flashlight with working batteries.

- An empty can and sanitary supplies for if you get stranded (use your imagination here).

- A high-calorie food option and some water.

- Candles and matches (for melting snow into water).

- Lock deicer (for helping you open your doors).

- Bottles of "ISO-HEET" fuel treatment or a similar product (to help prevent your fuel lines from freezing).

## Start Your Car and Let It Warm Up (but Not for too Long)

Now that your car and car kit are ready for winter, it's time for that Minnesota tradition—warming up the car. If you are a member of the lucky few with a remote car starter—a surprisingly common Christmas present in these parts—you can do so while in your pajamas! If you're like the rest of us, you get to hustle outdoors for a "sneak preview" of the weather.

Every winter a number of articles proliferate insisting that modern cars don't need to be warmed up because of advances in engine technology.[1] That much is true—older cars had carburetors (modern ones don't), and carburetors did need to warm up. But starting your car is important for a few reasons. First of all, oil thickens when it gets cold, and warming up your car helps warm up the oil. Without a good warm-up, you're putting an undue amount of stress on your engine.[2]

Now of course, this doesn't mean that you have to go bonkers with warming up your car. Half an hour is certainly excessive, as idling positively eats gasoline. Usually 5 or 10 minutes are sufficient, although your heat may not kick in fully until you're on the road. (But if you're dressed for the weather, it won't matter much.)

When you start your car, clear any snow/ice off your windows/windshield/mirrors and start your defroster (and your rear defroster if you have one). That way, when you get going, you'll be able to see. Driving with your mirrors or a rear window blanketed in ice or snow is dangerous, although it is sadly a common sight on the highways.

**Important Safety Note:** Only warm up your car in your driveway or on the street. Do not warm it up in a garage (even an open one) as wind can cause the carbon monoxide from the exhaust to "back up" into the garage (and into your house), making carbon monoxide poisoning a threat. Also, if you've stored your car outdoors for a long period of time, it's likely been surrounded by snow. Don't start it unless the undercarriage and exhaust system are clear (as the exhaust could back up). Of course, if you leave your car running with the keys in it, theft is a real concern; it's often handy to have an extra key (or fob), as this allows you to lock the car while it's running.

## Check the Forecast and Road Conditions

While your car is warming up, check the weather forecast and the road conditions. The Minnesota Department of Transportation reports on travel conditions on its website (http://lb.511mn.org/mnlb/) and the National Weather Service (or your local TV station) will give you a quick heads-up on the weather and what to expect. Many smartphone apps exist for this purpose, too.

## Bundle Up and Hit the Road

Before you head out the door, be sure to bundle up. If you depend on your car to stay warm, you could find yourself in a tight spot (and a cold one!) if your car dies.

Now that you're finally ready to go, here are some tips for winter driving:[1]

- There really is no substitute for winter driving experience. Thankfully, it's possible to practice. Finding an empty, icy parking lot usually works, although if you're driving aggressively or doing a lot of sliding, keep in mind that police could still ticket you. You can also just opt to try driving during a low-traffic time in areas where you know you'll be one of the only cars. Also, be especially careful after the first snowfall of the year, even if it's a small amount. Everyone seemingly forgets how to drive in snow, and that first storm usually serves as a rough reminder.

- Go slow. Speeding (or even going the speed limit in poor conditions) makes an accident more likely; also avoid using cruise control in winter.

- Use your seatbelt and stay off your cell phone; talking on the phone (or texting, which is illegal) is a bad enough idea when the weather's nice, but when the roads are bad, you really need to focus on driving.

- If there has been a storm, leave early and keep in mind that the busiest roads are generally plowed first. Roadways that see less traffic (including your neighborhood streets) are usually plowed later. This means that a highway may be in relatively drivable shape after a storm, but you may get stuck several times on unplowed neighborhood streets (or in your own driveway). Also keep in mind that not all counties have the same levels of resources when it comes to plowing, so if you notice a difference in the roads when you drive past the county line, that might explain it.

- If there is a lot of snow, and it's not plowed, the cars that have gone before may have made a path; follow it.

- On highways, there's often a "median" of snow in between the lanes. This makes getting over from one lane to another somewhat dicey (especially at 65 miles per hour). Be very careful when attempting to switch lanes, as this "median" can persist even when the rest of the road is mostly cleared.

- Watch out for bridges and overpasses, as they cool more quickly. They are more exposed to the weather, so ice forms there first; also be wary of turn lanes and intersections, as they are often ice rinks.

- When you're stopping or slowing, brake early and gradually. Sudden braking often will cause you to skid, and this can be a real problem. Turn lanes and stop signs are especially problematic. If you brake too hard, you'll slide right into the intersection.

- Don't pass another car if there is blowing snow (as you may not see oncoming traffic).

- If you find yourself sliding, don't panic. Take your foot off the gas and go with the slide if possible until you get some traction, then straighten out. If you have antilock brakes, don't pump the brakes, just use steady, gradual pressure.[2]

# Plowing and Plow Safety

## Whose Responsibility Is It to Plow?

From bustling four-lane U.S. interstates to lonely county roads, Minnesota has about 135,000 miles of roads and highways, and they all need to be plowed.[1] (For reference, the moon is about 240,000 miles from Earth.) A number of different entities are responsible for plowing all of these roads. The state's department of transportation is responsible for clearing interstates and state highways, counties clear off county roads, and cities/townships usually take care of their own streets/roads, unless they have an agreement or an understanding with the county.

## Plow Safety

Whichever entity is responsible for plowing in your area, stay safe around plows. A loaded plow weighs around 50,000 pounds, or about 15 times as much as the average car. You really don't want to hit one.[1]

### To Avoid an Accident, Take It from the DOT:[2]

- Yield to plows; they are big and you are not, and they go slower than the posted speeds

- Go slow

- Don't crowd a plow—or tailgate it; the DOT recommends staying five car-lengths back.

- Snowplows create snow clouds; don't drive into a snow cloud. A plow could be there and you could run smack into it.

## Road Salt and Why It Works

Snowplows deposit road salt and brine because it lowers the freezing point of water, helping to prevent ice formation from occurring and melting existing ice. Salt is more effective at warmer temperatures; as the temperature drops, the amount of salt needed increases, and its effectiveness decreases.[1] If it gets cold enough—below 15 degrees—even road salt has it limits, and snowplow operators are often forced to resort to other, more expensive chemicals. Under the wrong conditions—extreme winters with prolonged cold snaps, there isn't much that authorities can do until things warm up.[2]

## Where Does It Come From?

According to the USGS, about 30 percent of the salt used nationwide was used for road deicing, and the U.S. is actually one of the major producers of salt nationwide. What's bonkers is that some salt mines are beneath major U.S. cities.[1] Cleveland and Detroit are home to massive salt mines located 1,100 feet below the surface; the Detroit Salt Mine has operated for most of a century and spans some 1,500 acres.[2]

## More Than Just Sand and Salt

Snowplows don't just move snow, they also deposit sand or salt in key areas, as this helps prevent ice formation and help drivers maintain traction. But it's more than that. Snowplows often deposit less familiar substances on the roads in order to combat ice formation. One of the more popular options is liquid brine—a very salty solution that resists freezing, although other substances are used if conditions merit it.

## Road Salt and Water Quality

Unfortunately, while road salt is a necessity, all that salt has to go somewhere, and it often ends up in our lakes and rivers, which have been slowly becoming saltier over time.[1] This is doing damage to many water bodies in Minnesota, including a number of metro-area lakes, some of which—such as Brownie Lake—have been contaminated by deicing components.[2]

## Not So Simple after All

While we tend to think of snowplowing as being relatively simple, it's actually complicated. It involves a good deal of meteorology, local geography and chemistry, not to mention the insanely complicated logistics of coordinating activity on thousands of miles of roadways at the state, county and city (or even township) levels. So next time you see a plow driver, give them a friendly nod; or better yet, just stay back and stay safe.

# Common Winter Driving Problems

## So You Got Stuck in Your Own Driveway/Buried Your Car in a Snowbank

In winter, it's bound to happen—you'll get stuck, sometimes even in your own driveway. It's especially common after a storm has dropped a bunch of snow overnight. You'll wake up and get ready to leave the house only to find your driveway unplowed and your neighborhood streets a blanket of white. This can make it somewhat difficult to get out, especially if you don't have time to shovel or snowblow your driveway. Even if your driveway is cleared off, your neighborhood streets may not have been plowed yet.

## What to Do When You're Stuck

First things first, make sure you're OK; if it's just your driveway, you're probably fine, but if you buried your car in a ditch or spun out on the road, you may be injured or your car may be in a dangerous position (straddling two lanes, say). Don't get out of your car unless you think it's safe to do so. Look out for your immediate safety first, then work on getting out.

### Out on the Road

Put on your hazard lights, and make sure you've got your cold weather gear (and your shovel, you'll need it). Be careful when getting out as other cars could hit the same slick spot you did and smack into you. Walk around your car, preferably to the non-highway side, and ascertain how deeply your car is buried, and if you think you can get it out. Make sure your exhaust system isn't blocked by snow or ice; this can cause fumes to back up into the car.

- If you think your vehicle isn't buried too deeply, point your tires straight and try slowly reversing or going forward (depending on how your car is buried). If your car moves toward the road, continue moving in that direction. If you can help it, don't stop moving. (When it comes to getting unstuck, any motion is better than no motion.)

- If you have four-wheel drive available, use it.

  **Important:** Don't just gun the engine. The heat from the tires will melt troughs in the snow/ice, and you'll lose almost all traction unless your tires are actually on the asphalt. (This is also a great way to wreck your tires.)

If you come to a stop, that's not the end of the world—you're actually making progress. When you're stuck, movement (either forward or backward) is usually a good thing, as it clears out a space where your tires can get traction.[1] The trick is to "rock and roll" your car forward and backward until you get enough momentum to escape. This often involves short repeated shifts from "drive" to "reverse." The idea is to slowly rock the vehicle, enabling it to gain momentum and hopefully break free.

To help your car get traction, generously sprinkle some sand or kitty litter (from your car kit) beneath your car tires; if you do this, dig the area in front of the tires out. Placing cardboard or a wooden board can often work, too.

If you have people to help push, they'll want to push in sync with the rocking-and-rolling motion, as they'll help your car overcome the snow's hold. Of course, be very careful when reversing or accelerating a car when people are pushing your car; put the windows down and announce when you'll be reversing or advancing. If you're not comfortable driving, the folks helping you may be fine taking over.

If rocking and rolling isn't working, it's time to start digging. Other than the exhaust system, the first areas to clear of snow are the areas immediately in front of the tires and the undercarriage; when you get stuck, this often packs down snow tightly beneath the car, creating a "seal" that holds the vehicle there. Use a shovel or a (gloved!) hand to clear this out; a broom also works well, too (as you can push the snow through to the other side).

Keep in mind that if your car is well off into the ditch and all four wheels are buried, you'll probably need a tow truck or someone with a tow chain to get your car out. Bust out your cell phone and start dialing.

**IT COULD BE WORSE** As you might expect, car crashes are more common in slippery winter months (especially December and January), but perhaps surprisingly, deaths are more common in the warmer months (as more folks are on the roads and they are often going faster).[1]

## Avoiding Getting Stuck in the Driveway

- Check the forecast and get up early to shovel/snowblow your driveway; if the snow has already started falling and is forecast to do so until the morning, shovel whatever snow has fallen the night before. You obviously won't have a clear driveway when you wake up, but you'll make it easier to get out.

- If your driveway is covered in relatively deep snow and your car is in a garage, your car can act as a makeshift plow. But if you slow down or stop, that snow will build up beneath your undercarriage (and around your tires). So once you've committed to leaving the driveway, you should avoid stopping if possible. Obviously, be careful and don't go too fast or you could bury your car further or risk a crash.

- If you don't have a garage, you should at least shovel an escape path behind your vehicle; otherwise you may not be able to build up enough speed to get out.

- Garage or not, once you're on an unplowed road, you'll need to keep up a certain level of acceleration or else you'll get stuck there, too. I once helped a pizza delivery driver get unstuck three separate times in our cul-de-sac because they didn't maintain enough momentum.

- Stay home. That's only half a joke; if the weather is lousy and there's lots of snow, only go out of if it's necessary. Waiting a storm out (and letting the plow crews get caught up) is a great way to avoid getting stuck.

# So Your Door Lock (or Your Entire Handle) Is Frozen

Some types of precipitation (freezing rain, I'm looking at you!) can cause door locks, handles even entire doors to freeze solid. This is terrifically annoying, but thankfully, there are a number of ways to address this.

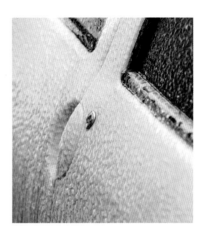

- If you can unlock your doors with a button on the remote, do it; after that, try the other doors (as they may not be frozen); this is especially true if one side of your car was shielded from the wind (and precipitation). If you can get in, success! Start your car and let it warm up and run the defrosters; then start scraping off the ice.

- Whatever you do, don't go to town or crank on the door handle, as that can break the door![1]

- If you are still having trouble, try chipping with an ice scraper (from your trunk or a pal's car).

- If the door isn't entirely frozen over and seems to be giving a bit, push it gradually with your body weight, this can often be enough to break the thin seal of ice holding it shut.

- If the door is still frozen, pick up some deicer from a gas station or a hardware store; there are DIY options as well.[2] Using warm water can work, but avoid boiling water, as the temperature differential can cause the glass to break.

- If your doors freeze up often, have your door seals checked out; these rubber gasket-like strips keep out moisture from outside; if they are broken or torn, water can get in and freeze.

# So Your Car Battery Died

It's one of the worst winter feelings: Your car doesn't start. Before you bust out your jumper cables, the first thing to do is to make sure it's your battery. If you turn the cabin lights on and they seem dim or you hear a clicking sound when you turn the ignition, it may be your battery.[1] If the lights aren't dim or the car attempts to turn over, then it may be something else.

If your battery is dead (or nearly so), be sure you know how to use jumper cables before trying to jump start a car. If you use them incorrectly, they can be dangerous or damage your car. Also, read your owner's manual; some cars have specific procedures for jump starting, and some cars (especially electric or hybrid cars) are a whole different situation.

- Wear safety gear (goggles and gloves); car batteries give off hydrogen gas, and they also consist largely of acid, so you don't want one blowing up in your face.

- You'll need to get the vehicles positioned so that the cables reach between both cars; if your car is blocked by another car or is in an awkward position, you may need to push it to make this possible.

- Once the vehicles are close enough for the cables to reach (but not touching), open the hood of both vehicles and turn off both (and all the electrical gizmos inside). Make sure you've got enough light to see the battery terminals on each vehicle. Battery terminals are color-coded; there are positive terminals, which are red, and negative terminals, which are black.[2]

- Lay out the cables on the ground, and don't touch the clamps together; like the battery terminals, jumper cables are color-coded, too.

- Connect the red cable to the positive terminal on the car with the dead battery; then connect the other red end to the positive terminal on the other car.[3]

- Connect the black cable to the negative terminal on the live car. Important: The next step is often overlooked; do not connect the other end of the negative cable directly to the dead car's negative battery terminal. Instead, connect it to an unpainted piece of metal within the engine, but away from the battery. This is important because car batteries produce hydrogen, and any spark could cause an explosion. (This happens more than you'd think.) If you've never done this, consult with a mechanic or someone who has.

- Once the cars are connected, back up and start the car with the charged battery. Wait a few minutes, then try starting the other car. If it doesn't work, turn off both cars and check the connections, as the clips can tend to slip, especially if the cables are stretched out. If that happens you may need to move the vehicles closer together (but never close enough for them to touch).

- Start the live car again, followed by the dead car after a few minutes. If the car starts, let it run for a few minutes (don't rev the engine, as that won't really help), and then disconnect the cables in this order: Remove the black (negative) cable from the formerly dead car, then the black (negative) cable from the live car. Then remove the red (positive) cable from the live car, and then the red (positive) cable from the dead car.

- Afterwards, be sure to have your battery checked out (and the terminals cleaned); if it happens often, you may need a replacement battery or have another mechanical issue.

> **It's Not Magic:** You might be thinking, how the heck does hooking up the negative cable to the car chassis work? As it turns out, the negative terminal on most batteries are electrically grounded through the chassis, so when you connect the negative clamp to a part of the engine, you're completing the circuit (and the battery receives the power). The only difference? There won't be any sparks near that potentially pesky hydrogen.

## Portable Jump Starting Kits

If you don't have jumper cables or if you know you'll be in area where you're not likely to find a running car to get a jump start, consider a portable battery kit. These suitcase-sized machines are essentially wall-charged jump start substitutes. You plug them in at home, then throw them in the trunk in case you need a jump. They have positive and negative clips, just like jumper cables, and they can be handy in a pinch (although they often run out of juice quite quickly). They often run 70 dollars and up. When using one, be sure to follow the instructions in the owner's manual.

# Winter Parking/How to Avoid Having Your Car Impounded

When the snow flies, plow drivers hit the roads, but they need a lot of space to do their jobs. This is especially true on the often narrow streets in major cities; this is why cities (even smaller ones) often have specific rules about where (and when) you can park in winter. When storms hit or are expected in the near future, cities issue snow emergencies, which often trigger very specific parking rules. So a word to the wise: Familiarize yourself with your area's parking rules and the city's snow emergency policies, and do so ahead of time. If you don't, you're liable to get a spendy ticket ($50 or more!) or, worse, have your car towed to the impound lot, which will run you several hundred dollars.

For Snow Emergency and Winter Parking Information

Minneapolis: www.minneapolismn.gov/snow/

St. Paul: www.stpaul.gov/snow

Duluth: www.duluthmn.gov/winterwatch/

Rochester: www.cityofrochester.gov/snowparkingrules/

Moorhead: www.cityofmoorhead.com

## If Your Car Is Impounded

In the metro, there are several different impound lots, so be sure to call ahead and figure out where your car actually is, what documentation you'll need to claim it (usually proof of ownership and proof of insurance). When in doubt, call ahead. There's nothing worse than going to the wrong impound lot or being turned away because you have the wrong paperwork. Some cities also have websites that allow you to search online for your impounded vehicle.

# Other Ways of Getting Around

Of course, you don't need a car to get around in the winter in Minnesota. Public transportation is a viable option throughout many of the state's major cities, and biking (yes, you read that right!) and walking (either outdoors or via the Minneapolis Skyway System) are also ever-popular options.

# Public Transportation
## In the Twin Cities

In the Twin Cities area, the Metro Transit system operates an extensive transportation system that includes buses, a light rail system in the Cities proper and a commuter rail system that reaches into the suburbs. This system doesn't stop during our winter, although delays and cancellations do sometimes occur.

Numerous park-and-ride options exist as well, enabling you to park close to home and skip the hassle of winter driving. (These park-and-rides often extend fairly far into the suburbs and exurbs.) Some larger employers (such as Target) also offer a discounted rate on Metropasses.

For more information, visit Metro Transit: www.metrotransit.org

## Outside the Metro

The Twin Cities isn't the only area with a public transit system; many of the state's larger cities have dedicated transit programs, and even less populated areas have some local transit options.

> Duluth: www.duluthtransit.com
>
> Rochester: www.rochestermn.gov
>
> St. Cloud: http://ridemetrobus.com
>
> Moorhead: www.matbus.com

For a complete list of public transit options in your area, visit www.dot.state.mn.us/transit/riders/

# Winter Biking

Yes, people bike during Minnesota winters. A lot of people do, actually. Minneapolis is an especially popular winter biking destination, as it features over 70 miles of dedicated biking trails and the city plows many trails. What's more, winter bike commuters are a common sight on city streets. If you're interested in getting around on two wheels in winter, visit www.minneapolismn. gov or www.thehubbikecoop.org to learn more. (Thanks to bike racks on city buses and the light rail, it's also easy to combine a bike commute with the rest of the Metro Transit system.)

Bikes with large, thick tires (known as fat-tire bikes) are becoming especially popular. True to their name, fat-tire bikes have thick, low-pressure tires and are designed to travel easily across snow or sand. These bikes were first popular with a core of diehard riders in the Twin Cities (many of whom took part in fat-tire bike races), but have since become popular nationwide.

When it comes to gear, the sky is definitely the limit, as there are many manufacturers of high-end bikes (with several manufacturers based here in Minnesota), but you can also find off-the-shelf gear at a more modest price.

Of course, given the weather, you need to dress warmly, and it's often helpful to have winter-specific gear. Bike shops sell specialized winter tires (and many riders even have a dedicated winter bike), and it's important to keep visibility in mind during the dark days of winter, so be sure to wear high-visibility gear and keep your cycle's lights in good working order. And given how hard winter biking is on the bike itself, it's important to stay up-to-date on regular maintenance. Certain varieties of chain grease can begin to gel up or freeze when it gets really cold out, so you may need to tweak your ride to make sure it's an option in the coldest weather. (Moreover, road salt is as rough on bikes as it is on cars, so be sure to wipe down your bike after a use. When you're getting started, it's often helpful to get your bike looked at by an expert.)

# Avoid the Outdoors Entirely:
# Skyway Systems in the Metro Area

Of course, walking is always an option, and if you're in Minneapolis you don't necessarily need to be bundled up to get from here to there. Minneapolis is home to the Minneapolis Skyway System, a network of enclosed walkways that spans 8 miles of downtown Minneapolis and connects many of the more prominent buildings, enabling you to get across downtown without ever stepping outside. The system is also a popular spot for dining and shopping. If you've never ventured through the Skyway before, take a little time to review the Skyway System Map (www.skywaymyway.com/), as the Skyway can be pretty confusing at first.

## St. Paul Skyway

The Minneapolis Skyway gets most of the press, but St. Paul (www.stpaulskyway.com) has a skyway system too. Clocking in at about 5 miles, St. Paul's system links much of downtown St. Paul. The St. Paul system is roughly grid-like and therefore easier to get around than Minneapolis's sprawling system.

## Gopher Way

The University of Minnesota is home to about 50,000 students, and it operates campuses in Minneapolis and St. Paul. Not surprisingly, many students prefer to avoid going outside in winter. In many cases, they get around using "Gopher Way," a system of tunnels and skyways that links many of the major University buildings. The University system is commonly divided into three portions: the East Bank, the West Bank and the St. Paul Campus. Both the East and West Banks are located in Minneapolis and divided by the Mississippi River. Each campus has its own tunnel/skyway system. Because getting around on campus sometimes means never going out-side, this can lead to classrooms full of students in sweatpants and flip-flops even when it's -20.

For more information, visit www1.umn.edu/pts/walk/gopherway.html

## Outstate Skyways and Tunnels

It gets cold elsewhere in Minnesota too, and other Minnesota cities have built their own systems to help pedestrians avoid the cold. Examples include Rochester, which boasts a skyway and a system of "subways" (underground tunnels) and Duluth, which has about 3.5 miles of aboveground tunnels. In addition, many universities also have skyways or tunnels to connect some of their buildings.

For more information, visit

Rochester Skyways/Subways: www.rochestercvb.org/go/getting-around/skyway-subway/

Duluth Skywalk: downtownduluth.com/skywalk/

# Enjoying the Snow

You don't just have to endure winter; you can enjoy it. And whether you're tromping around in the backyard on a winter hike or doing something more extreme—like ice climbing—there are many options to keep you active and entertained in the winter months.

# Build a Snowman

Do you want to build a snowman? No, that's a real question. (I have a toddler, so including a *Frozen* reference was required.) Snowmen, snowwomen and various snowpeople are often seen as solely a childhood pastime, but if you're from out of state, you may have never built one. So get to it! All you need is some sticky snow (the powdery stuff won't do the trick) to roll it into the characteristic snowman shape. Then comes the most important—and fun— part: accessorizing.

Now if this all seems a bit silly for "serious" adults, well, it is. But it's winter, and you've got to do *something*. Besides, we put all sorts of weird stuff in our yards in summer, when every neighborhood has that one yard with enough garden gnomes, flamingos and porcelain angels to invade a small nation. So why not decorate your yard with a custom snowman or a whole slew of them?

I prefer to make my snowmen/snowwomen a bit theatrical—one year we made snowmen and women for each member of the family (kids love this), and next year I'm thinking a pirate theme with cardboard swords and food dye and eye-patches would add some zest to the whole show. (Heck, if you get really into it, hold a competition with your neighbors, and award the winner with the most garish used trophy you can find at the thrift store.)

Besides, when the winter starts to grate on you, you get the fun of taking out your aggression on the snowmen. You can get pretty creative here. I've found that a snow shovel makes a handy impromptu scythe, and there's something to be said for a good full-on snowman tackle. So stay safe, have fun, and let winter have it.

# Make Snow Sculptures

If a snowman seems too childlike, consider making a snow sculpture. They actually aren't that hard to create. All you need is a design in mind (a castle? an animal? a flying saucer?), some basic tools (a spray bottle, a spatula, an ice cream scoop) and lots of slightly wet snow. If the snow isn't wet enough, you can add water with spray bottles.[1] While wearing warm gear, shape the general outline first, then set to work on the details. Whatever you make, make sure it can't topple over on you. You can then incorporate natural items (sticks and such), or you can use food coloring and the like to give your snow sculpture some pizzazz. To make it last longer, consider giving it an ice glaze by spraying it with a water bottle when you're done.

# Snow Forts and Snowball Fights

I'm a Minnesota boy, and I spent most of my childhood winters building snow forts and lofting snowballs. They are wintertime traditions and something I wholeheartedly recommend.

With that said, snow (especially wet snow!) is some heavy, heavy stuff, so you have to be careful when building snow forts. To help make things safer when building a snow fort or having a snowball fight, follow these tips:

- Avoid building a roof or digging tunnels, as these structures are liable to collapse.

- Don't build snow forts in heavy, wet snow.

- Stay away from the piles that snow-plows make; these are often prone to collapse and if you fall from one, you're liable to hit the street.

- If kids are at play, have an adult supervise and keep a shovel handy.

- If you have a snowball fight, be especially careful to avoid aiming at people's heads, and try to choose snow free of ice (ice balls hurt) or snow that might have rocks or gravel embedded in it. If you're going all out, consider wearing skiing goggles—you'd be surprised how many eye injuries are caused by snowballs each year.[1]

## Still Don't Believe Me? Here's the Math

I know what you're thinking: We built snow forts and it didn't hurt us. We're all fine! But that's not always true.[1] Here's a first-person example: I was briefly trapped under a collapsed snow tunnel when I was a kid. Thankfully, my head wasn't hit, but I was shocked at just how heavy the snow was on my legs. I couldn't move them and had to wriggle free to get out. Unfortunately, every year, there are incidents where folks don't turn out fine; kids are the most likely victims, but adults can even be at risk. In 2011, a Quebec man died in 2011 after a snow fort collapsed on him.[2] Given that there are easy ways to minimize risk, it's only prudent to take precautions, especially since kids are usually the ones at play.

I'm guessing some of you are still chafing at the above paragraph, however. If you don't believe me, here's the math. Let's say you make a snow fort with a roof that is 5 feet wide and long and about one foot thick, and let's say the snow is pretty average, not the crazy-heavy wet stuff we get in late February or March. A cubic foot of "normal" snow weighs perhaps 15 pounds, and just the roof of our structure would have a volume of 25 cubic feet. So if the whole shebang collapsed, that'd be 375 pounds, more than enough trap a child. And if you built a more ambitious snow fort or if its walls came down too, it'd be a lot heavier.[3]

The heavy, really sopping stuff can weigh even more, sometimes double that, so if you built the same snow fort above with heavy, wet snow, it might weigh more than 600 pounds. Tunnels can be even worse: if you dug a 7-foot-long tunnel that was 2 feet wide and had a roof 3 feet thick, it would have 42 cubic feet of snow above it. With heavy snow, that'd send 1,050 pounds of snow crashing down.

So by all means, build a snow fort, but do so safely.

## Sledding

We've got all that snow, so put it to good use. Minnesota may not be famous for mountains—let's be honest, at 2,301 feet, Eagle Mountain, our state's highest point, is a glorified hill—but that doesn't mean you can't enjoy sledding. Sledding is perhaps the most popular wintertime activity in the state, in part because it's so simple: all you need is snow, some warm gear, a sled, and a safe hill. (If you're a parent, the stamina to tramp up and down the hill after your kids

again and again.) Of course, you've got to keep things safe—getting your legs swept out from under you by a cackling ten year old hurts—and you've got to keep an eye out on icy jumps or hills that lead to streets, ponds or streams. But as far as winter fun goes, almost nothing beats sledding. It's cheap, fun, and there's almost no training required. If you haven't ever done it (or haven't since you were a kid), consider giving it a whirl.

# Downhill Skiing, Snowboarding and Tubing

Despite our general (OK, almost total) lack of mountains in Minnesota, skiing is a popular pastime, and the state has actually produced some champion skiers (paging Lindsey Vonn). There are over a dozen downhill ski facilities in the state and they feature a wide variety of ski runs, including everything from bunny hills to a few resorts with double-black diamond (expert) slopes, as well as the ski lifts to get you up the hill again.

Skiing gear is pretty specialized, and not everyone knows how to ski (or even how to put skis on), so skiing resorts in the state offer skiing lessons, gear rental, and slopes for all experience levels. The result is some of the best skiing in the Midwest; we may not be Vail or Aspen, but Minnesota skiing has quite a lot to offer.

Of course, not everyone heads to the slopes to ski. Snowboarding is a wildly popular sport, and most skiing resorts offer facilities for snowboarding as well, including some with terrain areas allowing you to try out the moves you may have seen in the Olympics or on the X-Games. Many sites also rent out boards and safety gear and offer lessons for beginners.

If skiing and boarding seem too tricky, consider tubing. Tubing basically consists of sledding on an inner tube, and some ski facilities feature hills specifically designated for tubing, and which feature rope-lines that take the work out of tramping uphill.

For a list of ski resorts in Minnesota, visit www.skiandboardmn.com or www.exploreminnesota.com

# Cross-Country Skiing and Snowshoeing

Of course, there's more than one way to ski, and Minnesota has some of the best cross-country skiing in the country. If you've never done it, cross-country skiing is exactly what it

sounds like—you ski along on a groomed trail and head across the landscape (not down it). There are two basic types of cross-country skiing: classic skiing and skate skiing. (Backcountry skiing is another option, but it requires specialized gear, and you ski in the absence of trails. For these reasons, it's more than a bit advanced, so I won't go into it in detail here.)[1]

Classic skiing and skate skiing are two different techniques to head down a groomed trail. In classic skiing, you lean forward to launch yourself ahead, using your ski poles to help propel you. In skate skiing, you use your skis more like rollerblades. Both use different gear/techniques to accomplish the same thing—and both are incredible ways to work out. (Cross-country skiing burns a lot of calories—an hour of moderate skiing burns well over 400 calories—and it's a wonderful way to see the state.)

If you don't have skis or groomed trails near you, don't worry, you don't need them! Snowshoeing is another great way to exercise and enjoy the outdoors; snowshoes don't cost all that much, and with just the sound of your footsteps echoing off of the snow, snowshoeing is a wonderful way to get away from the workaday world.

## Brightening up those Winter Nights: Ski by Candlelight

In winter, the days come early, and the seemingly endless darkness gets pretty old. That's what makes a ski trip by candlelight so enticing. The premise is just what it sounds like—state parks (and sometimes other organizations) line specific trails with candles or lanterns and hold a skiing event. These events are a lot of fun and produce some absolutely gorgeous pictures.

## Ski Races

If you really get into skiing, consider taking part in a ski race. Minnesota is home to some of the more prestigious ski races in the Midwest, including the Vasaloppet in Mora—named after the famous cross-country race of the same name in Sweden.

## Where to Start

If you've never gone cross-country skiing, head to a state park. Many state parks specifically groom trails for cross-country skiing, and some have rental equipment, offer cross-country lessons or even have lighted trails. What's more, many state forests, state parks, and city or county parks also offer groomed cross-country trails. Note, however, that you'll need a State Ski Pass when you're on state trails; thankfully, at $20, an annual pass isn't all that expensive.

For a map of state ski trails, visit: http://dnr.state.mn.us/skiing/skipass/map.html or www.dnr.state.mn.us/skiing/index.html

For a wealth of information about cross-country skiing, visit: http://mnnordicski.org/go-skiing/ or skinnyski.com

# Snowmobiling

You're not seeing things. There really may be mysterious headlights bobbing along in the ditches at night. If you're new to the area, seeing a snowmobile humming along beside you can be surprising. Minnesota boasts a positively insane number of snowmobiling trails; all in

all, there are over 22,000 total miles, nearly enough to circle the Earth. Snowmobiling is a fun, fast-paced pastime that has legions of adherents in the state. (Heck, I knew kids who rode them to school in the winter.) Better yet, there are thousands upon thousands of miles of dedicated snowmobiling trails in the state, and they crisscross almost every part of the state. Minnesota is even home to two snowmobile manufacturers—Arctic Cat and Polaris—and each has a rabid following (much like the Ford vs. Chevy camps).

The best way to start out snowmobiling is to contact your local snowmobiling club—there are dozens of clubs across the state, and they offer a wealth of information about the sport.[1] Before you go snowmobiling, you need to pass the state's snowmobile safety course. Available on CD, you can learn more by visiting the DNR link below.

You can also simply rent a snowmobile and the necessary gear. A number of resorts and motorsports stores (including one near the metro) rent gear, and they often offer guided tours and advice about how to operate the machines.

MN United Snowmobilers Association: www.mnsnowmobiler.org

Snowmobile Safety (MN DNR) www.dnr.state.mn.us/safety/vehicle/snowmobile/index.html

Snowmobile Rental information via Explore Minnesota: www.exploreminnesota.com

# Ice Fishing

You've seen it in the movies—some poor sap huddled atop a five-gallon bucket on a wind-swept frozen lake. You can ice fish like that, but many people opt to ice fish indoors, with heat, in their own purpose-built ice houses. These shelters often have doors (with locks), windows and even limited amenities. Some shelters boast a lot more; many "ice castles" offer sleeping areas and bathrooms, kitchenettes, and more. Some truly exceptional ice houses have full bars, satellite television, and more. There's even a bar in Zippel Bay that operates on the Lake of the Woods during the ice fishing season. What's more, many resorts also offer rental cabins or guide services that find the fish and drill the holes for you (and provide you with the gear). These make for great weekend trips.

This is what makes ice fishing so great—it's easy enough (and cheap enough) for the beginner to get involved, but the sky's the limit when it comes to amenities. Plus, don't forget the fish! A midwinter fish fry is a great way to liven up a January evening.

**A Safety Note:** Before you go fishing, it's very important to familiarize yourself with basic ice safety and what to do if you fall through. Also: Keep in mind that rivers, because they are in motion, don't always freeze over entirely, and even when they do, the ice may not be at all consistent. While no ice is 100 percent safe, river ice is especially suspect. For a good run-down of general ice safety, visit www.dnr.state.mn.us/safety/ice/index.html

# Hockey and Skating

From local outdoor rinks and ponds to year-round arena complexes, Minnesota is hockey and skating heaven. And you don't need to know how to skate to play, as there are hockey leagues for folks of all ages and skill levels, including boot hockey (played while wearing boots instead of skates), pond hockey (played on ponds or small lakes) and full-fledged recreational and competitive leagues. Hockey isn't the only way to enjoy the ice, either. Ice skating, speed skating, figure skating and curling are popular pastimes, too! Of course, as with ice fishing, you need to keep ice safety in mind.

If you want to join a league, ask around at your local arena or check out these links:

> Adult Hockey League (for beginners): www.ahahockey.com/programs/twin-cities/beginner-school
>
> Other Minnesota Hockey Leagues: www.activeminnesota.com/hockey

And if you're interested in watching hockey, you're in the right place. Minnesota is home to a wide variety of excellent hockey teams, including the Minnesota Wild NHL team, many top-ranked national men's teams (including the University of Minnesota, the University of Minnesota–Duluth, St. Cloud State University and Minnesota State Mankato) and the University of Minnesota women's hockey team. That's not to mention events like the Minnesota State Hockey Tournament and the U.S. Pond Hockey Championships.

> For more, visit
>
> Minnesota Wild: http://wild.nhl.com
>
> Minnesota State Hockey Tournament: www.mshsl.org/mshsl/activitypage.asp?actnum=410
>
> NCAA Division I Ice Hockey: /www.ncaa.com/sports/icehockey-men/d1
>
> U.S. Pond Hockey Championships (for spectators); www.uspondhockey.com

# Extreme Winter Fun

Like extreme sports? You're in the right state! The following is a description of just a few of the extreme winter options available to Minnesotans.

## Visit the North Shore

Minnesota boasts about 190 miles of Lake Superior's shoreline, and the North Shore is famous as a summertime destination thanks to its sweeping vistas, lighthouses, and the huge ships that visit many of Minnesota's ports. But Lake Superior is not to be missed in winter; portions of the lake freeze over every year, and in some winters, the entire lake freezes over. This is quite a sight in itself, as are the lake's ice-strewn beaches; the ice coats everything, and it can turn relatively ordinary beaches into sculptures that consist of plate glass. When the Big Lake freezes over, the region's sea caves are not to be missed, but they can only be safely visited when ice conditions are just right. See www.nps.gov/apis/mainland-caves-winter.htm for more information.

## Winter Camping

Some days, heading outside is its own variety of extreme sport, but some people opt to sleep outside, even when the weather is at its coldest. This is known as winter camping, and while it's not the most popular pastime, it's quite an experience. For more information, visit: www.dnr.state.mn.us/state_parks/winter_camping.html

## Fat-tire Biking

Want to go biking in the winter? On a frozen lake? Or across a field of unbroken snow? You can. Fat-tire bikes feature a specialized frame and rims, but it's the tires you'll notice first, thanks to their bulky, wide-bodied appearance. The tires on a fat-tire bike might even look "flat" and in a way, they are. Low tire pressure enables fat-tire bikes to ride atop snow, sand or other conditions where normal mountain bikes often have difficulty. Buying a fat-tire bike outright can be spendy, but some bike shops rent them, so check out http://ridefatbikes.com for more.

## Ice Climbing

When winter rolls around, the lakes aren't the only things that freeze. Our rivers also freeze over (although some sections stay open), and eventually, waterfalls even freeze over. In itself, this is a weird, wonderful sight, but it gets even cooler once you see folks ice climbing. Ice climbing is exactly what it sounds like: using mountain climbing gear to scale the frozen face of a waterfall. You have to know what you're doing, have the proper gear and you need to acquire

permission to climb in a given area (climbing Minnehaha Falls, for example, is illegal). But ice climbing makes for an incredible experience (and wild photos). To get started, contact your local outdoors outfitter. Some outfitters, especially on the North Shore, rent ice climbing gear or offer training sessions. Or visit the Sandstone Ice Fest, an ice climbing festival held every year in Sandstone. It offers ice climbing clinics, as well as a dedicated "ice park" for winter climbing.

Other ice climbing options exist, especially on the North Shore, so be sure to contact your local rock climbing group or store, for more information. You can also hone your climbing skills in summer at the Minnesota State Park system's "I Can Climb!" programs.

For more information:

Sandstone Ice Fest: www.sandstoneicefest.com

Information on Ice Climbing in Minnesota:
www.mountainproject.com

I Can Climb Program (held in Summer):
www.dnr.state.mn.us/state_parks/ican/climb.html

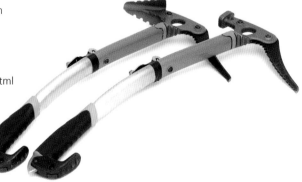

## Ice Boating

Powered by the wind, ice boats skim along the surface of a frozen lake by essentially riding along on a pair of skates. Because many lakes are positively windswept, ice boats can reach impressive speeds—upwards of 50 miles per hour—providing a real winter thrill. With that said, ice boating is risky. Lake ice is fickle stuff, and it doesn't always freeze consistently across the lake. Since ice boats can cover a lot of ice, it makes it more likely you'll encounter lousy ice, increasing the danger. So it's incredibly important to take safety precautions and to analyze ice conditions.

To learn more, visit: www.iceboat.org

## Polar Plunge

When just going outside is cold enough to cause you to utter a few choice words, you might think that a polar plunge—jumping into a frozen lake—might seem nuts. And who am I kidding? It is sort of nuts, but in a good way. These so-called polar plunges or polar bear plunges are often held to raise funds for charity (often the Special Olympics) and feature all sorts of folks (sometimes dressed in costume) jumping into a small section of lake where ice has been cut out. At these fairly large events with a variety of safety precautions in place, plungers are assisted by staff members wearing cold-water immersion suits, and medical staff are on hand, just in case. After the jump, there are warming houses and hot drinks to help jumpers warm up. Such plunges are certainly a way to liven up your average winter weekend. As for what it's like: there is no real way to describe it. You'll just have to try it yourself.

To find a plunge near you, visit: www.plungemn.org

# The Holiday Season

They don't call it the holiday season for nothing. From Christmas light festivals and the Christmas train to Hanukkah and Kwanzaa celebrations, the holidays are jam-packed with festivities. Here's a brief list of just a few holiday-themed festivities in Minnesota.

## Murphy's Landing

A historic look at the holidays in Minnesota, Murphy's Landing in Shakopee is complete with costumed reenactors, carriage rides, music and more. For information, visit www.threeriver-sparks.org

## The Canadian Pacific Holiday Train

Every year, the Canadian Pacific Holiday Train visits Minnesota, stopping at several sites across the state.[1] Decked out in Christmas lights, the train isn't just for show—it collects donations for charity, often area food shelves. And there's more than just the treat of a train covered in lights. Each time it stops, musicians on board put on a holiday concert. To see where it stops, visit, www.cpr.ca/holiday-train/canada

## Christmas Lights

When it comes to those who put up Christmas lights, some folks put up a few strings and a wreath and call it good, but others go all-out. Whether it's a quick spin around the neighborhood or a dedicated trip to a house (or block) with tricked-out Christmas light displays, it wouldn't be winter without a trip to see some Christmas lights. Because display locations often change (it's a lot of work to put up thousands of lights, year by year), the Internet is the best resource for up-to-date information; www.prairielights.info is a good starting point.

## Hanukkah

Hanukkah, also known as the "Festival of Lights," lasts for eight days and is held to commemorate the improbable victory of the people of Israel against an ancient enemy and the subsequent recapture/rededication of the Holy Temple.[1] Its most famous symbol is the menorah, a candelabra; one candle is lit each night, until the entire Menorah is lit on the eighth night. Because Hanukkah's dates are based on the Jewish calendar, its dates vary on the Gregorian calendar, although it often falls entirely in December.[2] If you'd like to learn more about Hanukkah, check the area papers, as they often list Hanukkah happenings. Or give your local synagogue a call to see if they are hosting an event related to Hanukkah.

## Kwanzaa

Kwanzaa is another popular holiday in Minnesota. Celebrated from December 26 until January 1, Kwanzaa is a celebration of Pan-African culture that is especially popular among Minnesota's many African-Americans. With its name stemming from the Swahili word for "first fruits," the holiday is based upon seven core principles of African culture: unity, self-determination, collective work/responsibility, cooperative economics, purpose, creativity and faith.[1] Kwanzaa events are held every year, so check the local papers for event locations and dates.

## The Lunar New Year

The date of the New Year falls on January 1 under the Gregorian calendar, which is a calendar based on the movement of the Earth around the sun. Nonetheless, historically, many calendars have been based on lunar cycles, and the Chinese calendar is among them. This calendar is popular across much of Asia, and while official business is done with the Gregorian calendar, holidays are often honored according to the lunar calendar. Perhaps the most well-known example is the Lunar New Year, which occurs in January or February of each year.[1] The holiday is celebrated by folks across the country, including many here in Minnesota. Celebration sites and dates vary each year, so check the news and the web, and join the fun.

# Fun Winter Festivals

You don't have to stay indoors for the winter, you really don't. Many cities and towns hold winter festivals that are fun for the whole family and that make for a great way to break up the winter monotony. The following list just scratches the surface of wintertime in Minnesota.

## St. Paul Winter Carnival (www.wintercarnival.com)

In 1885, a New York reporter visiting St. Paul in the winter cracked that the city was "another Siberia, unfit for habitation." This didn't sit too well with the residents of that libeled city, and in an act of defiance they held the first winter carnival. The carnival has been held dozens of times since, with yearly carnivals occurring every year since 1946. Held in January and February, the carnival has a mythology all its own and features parades, treasure hunts, good food, races and occasionally full-fledged ice palaces. (One of these palaces even figured into a short story by St. Paul native F. Scott Fitzgerald.)

## Art Sled Rally (http://artsledrally.com)

The Twin Cities are an arts hotspot, so is it really that surprising that we incorporate art into our winter fun? The Art Sled Rally is exactly what it sounds like—a gathering of "art sleds" in Minneapolis's Powderhorn Park. So start working on that Van Gogh-themed sled!

## Eelpout Festival (www.eelpoutfestival.com)

Eelpout aren't exactly the most sought-after fish in Minnesota. In fact, eelpouts have a decidedly negative reputation, as they are slimy, eel-like fish that have a disconcerting tendency to wrap themselves around an unsuspecting angler's arm. (They aren't nicknamed "lake lawyers" for nothing.) Relatives of the cod, they are actually an underrated catch, as they are delicious and can be huge. Every January (at the height of eelpout mating season), Walker, Minnesota, hosts an eelpout festival on Leech Lake, complete with fishing, contests, eelpout curling and more.

### Ice Climbing Festival (www.sandstoneicefest.com)

Want to learn how to ice climb? Head to Sandstone, where the famous Ice Festival is held each December. It's a great way to learn from the pros about a sport that is gaining in popularity.

### Icebox Days (http://ifallschamber.com/icebox-days/)

International Falls is known as the Icebox of the Nation, and every January it embraces that moniker by hosting Icebox Days, which features the "Freeze Yer Gizzard Blizzard Run," snow sculpture competitions, turkey bowling and more.

### John Beargrease Sled Dog Marathon (www.beargrease.com)

The name "John Beargrease" is synonymous with the North Shore. Beargrease was an Ojibwe Indian who carried mail between Two Harbors and Grand Marais—a round-trip of over 160 miles.[1] He used a variety of different methods to deliver mail but is most famous for traveling by dogsled in winter.

The John Beargrease Sled Dog Marathon is held in his honor, and covers almost 400 miles.

### Other Festivals

This list is far from definitive; many cities hold their own winter festivals. Examples include Duluth (http://twinportswinterfest.com) and Rochester (www.rochesterwinterfest.com), so when in doubt, check the web or your papers for more information.

# Snow Days, Snowy Science Projects and Getting the Heck out of Dodge

If you can't go outside (or just plain don't want to), then the question arises: What should you do to pass the time? Thankfully, if you're creative, there are all sorts of fun ways to enjoy a cold (or snowy) winter's day. And if all else fails, you can head somewhere warmer!

# Winter Science Projects

Our winters may be cold, but with these cool (literally!) winter science projects you can put the weather to good use!

## The Famous Boiling Water Trick

When it gets really cold, you might see the TV weatherman or a neighbor chuck a pot of boiling water out the window. What happens might surprise you—the water instantly turns to a cloud of snow. (This is especially dramatic if it's really cold and the water is thrown from a great height.) According to climatologist Mark Seeley, cold air is often quite dense and very dry, so it has little ability to carry water vapor. Boiling water is practically spewing water vapor, so it has nowhere else to go and precipitates out as snow. If you want to try this at home, keep in mind that the effect is more dramatic if it's colder, and you need to take proper precautions—wear safety gear and be darn sure about the wind direction when you throw the water. A surprising number of people are burned each year while trying this.

## Grow Your Own Snow[1]

If you don't want to venture outside, you can grow your own snowflakes—in your kitchen. Now, I know what you're thinking—you've got enough of the stuff in your driveway—why would you ever want to bring any more snow into the world?! First of all, it's a wonderful way to introduce kids to the basics of meteorology. It's also cheap, relatively easy and plain-darn fascinating.

The following experiment is adapted with permission from Caltech physicist Kenneth Libbrecht's wonderful website about snowflakes (www.its.caltech.edu/~atomic/snowcrystals/). For an in-depth look at snow, also be sure to pick up his outstanding book, *Kenneth Libbrecht's Field Guide to Snowflakes*.

## Supplies

> An empty, clean 20-ounce plastic pop bottle
> 3 large-diameter Styrofoam cups
> A small, round kitchen sponge (a half-inch thick)
> A short length of nylon fishing line (thinner is better, say, one-pound test)
> A strong sewing needle
> 4 straight pins
> A paper clip
> Some paper towels
> 10 pounds of dry ice (in a Styrofoam cooler)
> 2 plastic grocery bags
> A hammer
> A piece of cardboard

**Step 1:** Use a sharp knife to cut the bottle in two, about a half inch above the bottom. Poke a hole in the center of the bottle bottom using a knife or the needle, and also poke four holes in the side of the bottle bottom. Then fit the sponge inside the bottle bottom, and hold it place by placing pins into the side holes.

**Step 2:** Thread the fishing line into the sewing needle, and push the needle through the hole in the bottle bottom and up through the sponge. Attach the fishing line to the bottle bottom with a piece of tape, and tie a knot in the other end to the paper clip. When the pop bottle is inverted and reassembled, the string should swing freely inside the bottle.

**Step 3:** Place the inverted bottle inside the three Styrofoam cups, so that the bottom of the bottle label is at the same height as the top of the cups. There should be about one inch of clear space between the sides of the pop bottle and the top edge of the Styrofoam cups.

**Step 4:** Now it's time to cool things down; that's where the dry ice (solid carbon dioxide) comes in. (To buy some, check the Internet or the yellow pages.) Keep in mind that dry ice is quite cold, so you'll need to wear gloves when touching it. You'll notice that the dry ice appears to "steam" when exposed to the atmosphere; that's occurring because it's undergoing sublimation—it's changing from a solid to a gas. Under normal atmospheric pressure, carbon dioxide doesn't have a liquid phase. Pull the top off the chamber (the bottle bottom and the sponge), wet the sponge with tap water, and replace.

**Step 5:** Put the dry ice inside two plastic grocery bags, and pound on it with a hammer to crush the dry ice. This works best on a hard surface, but it's not very hard to do, as dry ice isn't nearly as tough as water ice. Put the crushed dry ice back into its Styrofoam cooler, and use a spoon to transfer some into the Styrofoam cups around your chamber. Fill the cups to the top, and cover with a piece of cardboard cut to shape or with some paper towel strips. (Wrap some paper towels around the top of the Styrofoam cups, as well. Be sure to add as much dry ice as you can to the cups, and add more dry ice every so often. (If the experiment doesn't work, it's probably because the dry ice level is too low.)

**Step 6:** Observe! Small ice crystals should begin forming on the string after 5 to 10 minutes, and after an hour you should have a pretty good bunch of crystals. When things get crowded, you can pull the top off the chamber, wipe the string clear with your fingers, and try again. You should also knock the crystals off the walls of the chamber; swinging the paper clip around accomplishes this nicely. One "charge" of dry ice will last about 6 hours, and more can be added as needed.

**Step 7:** Take pictures and compare your snowflakes with those you've seen outside! How do they compare? What might explain the differences?

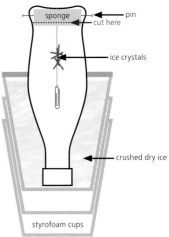

## Designer Snowflakes

Growing your own snowflakes isn't just a do-it-yourself science project. Researchers at Caltech and other universities have created artificial snowflakes in the laboratory.[1] The study of crystals—including those found in snowflakes—is called crystallography, and it's important for a number of reasons, as it has potential applications in a wide variety of fields, including materials research and chemistry. In a real respect, that's the fun part of science—you never know where one discovery will be applied next.

> **Another fun project with dry ice:** While you're at it, purchase a bit more dry ice than you need; it figures into another neat DIY science experiment called a cloud chamber, which you can use to detect cosmic rays (high energy particles from supernova and other astronomical events). For instructions just head on over to Google; for one resource, see the Recommended Reading section on page 167. Growing your own snowflakes and high-energy physics on the same day—what's cooler than that?

## Freeze a Bubble

If the conditions are right, you can freeze a bubble. The results are positively otherworldly—all the beauty of a bubble but locked in place, almost like a tiny sculpture. The best way to do this is to make your own bubble mix consisting of the following:[1]

6 cups water
1 cup light corn Syrup
2 cups (16 ounces) clear dish washing liquid

Head outdoors, and blow bubbles. If you can, gently try to get them to land on a cleared area; eventually one will stick and freeze. Or you can snag a "normal" bubble on the wand, and let it freeze. Obviously, the colder it is, the better. Then bust out the camera.

### Freeze Bubbles but Avoid the Cold

You can also freeze bubbles without ever going outside. Do so by coating a plate in bubble solution, then blow a bubble gently onto the plate. Gently separate it from the wand (this takes some doing) and transfer the plate to a pre-cleared area in the freezer. Keep in mind that this is pretty tricky to do—I succeeded last year, but only after a dozen tries or so. Leave the bubble, undisturbed, and it'll freeze.

## Photograph Snowflakes

If you want to get high-quality photos of snowflakes, all you need is a digital camera, a black piece of fleece that you've left outside for 30 minutes or so (to get it nice and cold) and some snow. Flakes will land on the black scarf, giving your photos a nice contrast; to get the best shots, use a macro lens (if you have one) or your macro setting on your camera. A flash helps in poor light conditions. The variety of snowflakes will surprise you, and you should be able to get some great shots!

## Collect Snowflakes

With some super glue, some microscope slides and a bit of effort, you can actually preserve and collect(!) snowflakes.[1] The first thing you'll need is some super glue, which should be nice and watery (not gel-based). Leave the slides and covers outside until they are the same temperature as the air. Collect falling snowflakes with a piece of cardboard, then use a magnifying glass to find a nice specimen. Pick it up with a small artist's paintbrush (this can be tricky) and put it on one of the slides. Put a drop of super glue on the snowflake, then put the cover on top. Leave it outside for a few weeks (or throw it in the freezer). The glue will harden, preserving a "fossil" of the snowflake. If you do this, you can create your own collection of snowflakes.

### Enjoy Some Movies with Minnesota Connections

With all of our snow and ice, you'd think that Minnesota would have a disproportionate amount of movie critics. After all, winter is a perfect time to get caught up on your movies. The following are some of the more well-known movies either set in Minnesota or filmed here.[1]

*Grumpy Old Men* (and sequels)

*Mighty Ducks*

*Miracle*

*Fargo* (filmed mostly in Brainerd)

*Jingle All the Way* (features St. Paul's famous Mickey's Diner)

*A Prairie Home Companion*

*Field of Dreams*

*Contagion* (set in Minnesota)

Anything by the Coen Brothers (born in St. Louis Park)

## Good Food for Cold Days: Food and Drinks

I don't know about you, but when it gets darn cold, hearty, spicy foods are the order of the day. Here are a few of my favorite hot-and-spicy wintertime food options.

### Buffalo Wings

I'm a buffalo sauce fanatic. I could practically bathe in the stuff. As you might expect, Buffalo wings get their name from their birthplace—Buffalo, NY—which is no stranger to snow (and a lot of it!). Like most momentous events in human history, the story of the invention of the buffalo wing is a bit convoluted, but all parties agree that it was invented at the Anchor Bar, at a time when chicken wings were viewed as little more than a waste product.[1] They soon caught on, however, and now there are wing joints around the world.

This is my adaptation of the original recipe from the Anchor Bar.[2]

> 36 chicken wings (this will serve about 4 people)
> 4 teaspoons vegetable oil
> 1 teaspoon salt
> ¾ cup flour
> 1 stick butter
> 4 teaspoons cider vinegar
> ¼ to 1 teaspoon cayenne pepper
> ⅛ teaspoon garlic powder hot sauce

Buffalo wings are customarily served with celery sticks and blue cheese dressing, but I can't stand celery, so I usually spare it. Carrots are a nice replacement, and experiment with other dressings as you see fit.

1. Set oven to 425.

2. Put wings in a large bowl, then toss them with the oil and the salt. Sprinkle flour over the wings, then bake them on a large foil-covered cookie sheet for 20 minutes. Flip 'em, then bake another 20 minutes. In the meantime, wash the large bowl, as you'll be needing it again.

3. To make the sauce, mix the butter, the vinegar, the pepper, and the hot sauce until it simmers.

4. Once the wings are done, put them back in the large bowl and dump the sauce over them. Then serve 'em up!

These wings are definitely not healthy, but they are oh-so-amazing, and if you're making this for two, you'll have extras! In my book (literally!) cold wings are almost as good as cold pizza. Almost.

## Pho

Pronounced "fuh," Pho is a Vietnamese soup that often features beef broth and noodles. (There are many, many different ways to make it, however.) However you make it, it's one of those perfect wintertime foods, as it's hearty, warm and often spicy. Making pho at home takes time—to prepare pho, you need to simmer the broth for hours—so if you've got a hankering for some on the quick, check out one of the dozens of restaurants in Minnesota.

If you want to try making your own at home, check out the recipe listed in the references section on page 166. Or, visit the web and check out the best-reviewed restaurants for pho in the Twin Cities.[1]

## Baseball Food

My wife and I take baseball pretty seriously. Sure, we love the sport, but if you're from Minnesota, baseball encompasses the best weather Minnesota has to offer, and the phrase "pitchers and catchers report to spring training" tend to become more than just a reference to pre-season baseball. Even though it occurs in February, when the weather is still plenty awful, the phrase heralds winter's eventual demise. That's why my wife and I always hold a baseball-themed party in February. Sure, there's almost always snow on the ground, and you have to tramp through the snow to get to the grill, but none of that matters.

We usually make the following:
> Cheese-filled turkey brats (relatively healthy) along with condiments
> Nachos (we like the Salpica Ballpark Nacho cheese sauce, which comes in a little pouch)
> Pretzels (found in the freezer section)
> Malt cups

## Lebkuchen, Lefse and Other Treats

Of course, winter is replete with treats. It's easy to understand why: There's an old saying—I first heard it at a grocery store from a woman who looked to be in her sixties—when you're snowed in, there are only two things you can do. One is to bake cookies. The other is a bit more off-color. As it turns out, she's not the only one to think that; when it comes to when the stork arrives in Minnesota, the months of July, August, and September are especially common months for new arrivals. Scientists don't know if the old anecdote is true, but hospitals regularly prepare their delivery rooms 9-10 months later after a big cold snap hits.[1] This is all a long-winded way of saying: Winter is a great time to bake!

Some of my favorite options include Lebkuchen, a gingerbread recipe from Germany, lefse sprinkled with sugar and cinnamon (you can pick lefse up at many grocery stores) and homemade ice cream, using Minnesota's cold weather in place of a freezer or an ice-cream making machine.

## Homemade Ice Cream (Made Outdoors)

First thing's first, it needs to be cold. Fifteen or twenty below are ideal. (There's a sentence I didn't think I'd ever say.) The first thing you need to do is to make your ice cream mix; here is a simple ice cream recipe, which is adapted from the website *The Special Fork*.[1]

> ¾ cup sugar
> ¾ cup water
> 1 cup milk
> 1 cup heavy cream
> ¼ teaspoon salt
> ½ teaspoon vanilla

1. Combine the sugar with the water in a small pot and whisk over medium heat, just until sugar is dissolved. Pour into a large heatproof bowl and cool completely.

2. Add milk, cream, salt and vanilla to the bowl and combine.

3. Then place the bowl in the refrigerator until it chills. In the meantime, place a metal bowl large enough to hold the ice cream mix outside. (As anyone who has grabbed the metal handle of a pan on the oven knows, metal conducts heat/cold quite well, so it'll help the ice cream batter get colder faster.)

4. Once the bowl has been outside long enough to be at air temperature, spoon out the ice cream mix into the bowl.[2] Let it sit outside until it begins to freeze at the edges (this often takes 45 minutes to an hour), then stir the mix for a minute or two. Repeat this process until the ice cream becomes too difficult to stir. Ice cream gets its wonderful smooth texture because it is churned as it freezes. If it weren't, it'd freeze in one block. That's why ice cream machines stir the ice cream constantly as it freezes. Usually the ice cream will need four or five separate "churning sessions" before it's finished, though this depends on the temperature.

5. Once the ice cream is finished, move it to a container and place it the freezer. When you're ready to serve it, leave it out to soften up a bit, then enjoy. (Again, keep in mind that the colder the weather, the better; if it's warmer, you're more likely to get a milkshake-like mix, but it'll still taste good).

> **Note:** If you don't want to head outside, you can also use an ice cream maker to make this recipe.

> **Now a little science:** Why do many do-it-at-home recipes have you submerge a bag or a sealed canister of ice cream mix amid rock salt, ice and briny water? Well, salt lowers the freezing point of water, and submerging the ice cream amid this mixture makes it freeze more quickly. This recipe removes the middleman, having the not-so-great outdoors provide the cold and you provide the manual labor. If your first batch of ice cream doesn't turn out, tinker with the recipe (or try again at different temperatures); it's a great way to make science literally sweet. You can also add various flavorings and additions as you see fit.

## A Few Beverages

Of course, when it gets really cold, ice cream just won't cut it. You need something warm to drink.

### Hot Chocolate

I'd be remiss if I didn't mention that wintertime standard—hot chocolate—in this book. Whether you opt for the comfort food of Swiss Miss or make your own, it's never a bad idea to keep a bunch on hand.

### Peppermint Patty

If you're of legal drinking age, a peppermint patty is one way to spice up hot chocolate. All you need is some schnapps, some crème de menthe, some crème de cacao, hot chocolate and whipped cream.[1] Many recipes call for an ounce of schnapps, half an ounce of crème de cacao and a teaspoon of crème de menthe. (For reference, a shot glass holds about an ounce and a half of liquor.) I rarely measure these ingredients all that precisely, instead winging it as my mood (and the wind chill) dictates. Making it is easy; mix the liqueurs together, and then add them to the hot chocolate and cover it with whip cream.

## Hot Toddy

The Hot Toddy is another wintertime standard, and it's a perfect nip after a long slog against the snowdrifts in the driveway.

> One shot's worth of brandy or rum
> 1 tablespoon of honey
> The juice from one lemon wedge
> A cup of tea (tea bags are fine)

Making it is easy: Put a tablespoon or more of honey in a mug, followed by the liquor and the lemon juice. Make a cup of tea (plain old Lipton works fine, though fancier stuff works too), then pour the tea into the honey-liquor mix, stirring well.

**IT COULD BE WORSE** During Robert Falcon Scott's ill-fated trek to the South Pole (his party perished on the return voyage), he and his men man-hauled their sledges across the inhospitable Antarctic terrain. They did so without a real working knowledge of the nutritional requirements of such a voyage; a modern analysis of their trip suggests that at its most demanding, they burned 11,000 calories per day, more than that burned by Tour de France bikers.[1] Unfortunately, they only ingested a maximum of 4,600 calories, far lower than needed to compensate for the energy they lost due to the cold and the drudgery of pulling a sled across the barren snows. (Man-hauling a sled with the appropriate amount of calories for such a trip is actually impossible.) This caloric deficit triggered a deadly cycle: Cold leads to energy expenditure, which depletes energy reserves, leading to decreased heat retention. This causes muscle loss, exposing one to the elements longer, leading to more heat loss. Even today, man-hauling a sledge to the South Pole is just as the cusp of the possible.

# Get the Heck out of Dodge

While there are many ways to enjoy the winter, sometimes snowbirds have the right idea. Eventually, you might reach a breaking point and feel the urge to flee for warmer climes, if only temporarily. You're not alone. As someone who has fled the state solely because of winter on several occasions, here are my winter getaway recommendations.

## Arizona or Florida?

Arizona and Florida are two ever-popular destinations for Midwesterners trying to avoid the cold. Southern Arizona is famous for its deserts and "dry heat" whereas Florida is synonymous with spring break, Jimmy Buffet and margarita weather. As it happens, because Minneapolis-St. Paul International Airport is a hub for international airlines, both options are relatively affordable, as long as you plan ahead.

## Brett's Travel Tips (Based on My Visits to Both Areas)

- It often helps to get your tickets ahead of time, especially if you're flying on a smaller air carrier. Always check last-minute deals, too, and if your travel plans are flexible, it's always helpful to consider flying into different airports and selecting flights on different days. Florida has more major airports than Arizona, but Arizona's two major airports (Phoenix and Tucson) offer quite a few flights.

- Once you're on the ground, however, Florida can be darned expensive, especially if you're planning on visiting its famous theme parks. (One way to assuage this is by getting a package deal; if you do so, you may be able to get tickets at a much discounted rate.) If you'll be driving keep in mind that Orlando also has a *lot* of toll roads.

- If you're like me, you love baseball, and both states have a lot to offer for the wintertime traveler, as each state is the site of one of Major League Baseball's spring training leagues. The Grapefruit League is based in Florida, and the Cactus League is based in Arizona. If you're a Twins fan, head to Fort Myers, as that's where the Twins play their winter ball. And even if you're not a baseball fan, check a game out; the atmosphere is markedly less formal, the seats are cheap, and if you hang around, you might be able to actually meet some of your favorite players.

- The scenery in both states couldn't be more different—so this is just a matter of taste. Arizona's deserts, mountains and highlands offer more variety than you'd think (though be aware that northern Arizona can be surprisingly cold; I was once snowed in at Flagstaff). The same goes for Florida, of course; in January, temperatures can occasionally dip into the 40s. As for the rest of the state, it's not all beaches and palm trees; once you head into the interior of the state, you'll find a swampy, strange place. And did I mention the alligators? (No, really, you'll probably see alligators.)

- Both states offer a wide variety of ways to enjoy the (warm!) outdoors. In Arizona, you can hike, mountain climb and golf to your heart's content. In Florida, you can fish, swim and even kayak with manatees.

**"Snowbird" Is Not Just a Nickname:** We're all familiar with real-life snowbirds—birds that spend the warmer months in one area, then migrate south during the winter. The Arctic tern is the champion of the snowbirds and takes this tendency to the limit. It spends its summers in the Arctic, and its winters near Antarctica. All in all, it travels over 20,000 miles a year and probably sees more daylight than any other creature on the planet.[1]

# Resources/References

### What to Expect Month by Month in the Twin Cities

### Monthly Averages

National Centers for Environmental Information. "Summary of 30 Year Monthly Normals for Minneapolis St. Paul International Airport, 1981-2010." Data compiled by via Minnesota Climatology Working Group, and accessed via http://climate.umn.edu/pdf/normals_means_and_extremes/msp_normals_1981-2010.pdf

### Snowfall Averages and Snowiest Months on Record

National Oceanographic and Atmospheric Administration. "*Local Climatological Data – Annual Summary with Comparative Data.*" Accessed via Normals, Means and Extremes for Minneapolis (KSMP), "30 year Normals (1981-2010)" from the Minnesota Climatology Working Group at http://climate.umn.edu/pdf/normals_means_and_extremes/msp_normals_means_extremes_page3.pdf

### Monthly Snow Records

The National Weather Service, Twin Cities/Chanhassen. "Top Ten Snowfalls Per Month," Data compiled by the Minnesota Climatology Working Group and accessed via http://files.dnr.state.mn.us/natural_resources/climate/twin_cities/monthsno.html

### Understanding Minnesota Winter

1. Minnesota Climatology Working Group. "Minnesota Climate Extremes." www.dnr.state.mn.us/climate/summaries_and_publications/extremes.html

### Length of Day

1. Time and Date AS. "Minneapolis, U.S.A. — Sunrise, sunset and day length, 2015." Accessed via www.timeanddate.com/world-clock/sunrise.html

### Growing Pains (The First/Last Frost)

1. National Climactic Data Center. "Final Spring/First Fall Freeze & Frost Date Probabilities." Data compiled by the Minnesota Climatology Working Group and accessed via www.dnr.state.mn.us/climate/summaries_and_publications/freeze_date.html

### How Long Is Snow on the Ground?

1. National Weather Service. "MINNEAPOLIS/ST PAUL INTERNATIONAL AIRPORT, EXTREMES OF SNOWFALL." Data compiled by the Minnesota Climatology Working Group and accessed via http://climate.umn.edu/doc/twin_cities/snowvar.htm

### Ice-In and Ice-out Dates

1. Minnesota Climatology Working Group. "Median Lake Out In Dates, 1950-2015." Accessed via www.dnr.state.mn.us/ice_out/index.html?year=median

2. Minnesota Climatology Working Group. "Median Lake Ice In Dates, 1950-2015." www.dnr.state.mn.us/ice_out/index.html?year=median

### It Could Be Worse: Historical Ice-out Dates

1. Minnesota Climatology Working Group. "Minnesota's Historical Lake Ice-Out Dates."

http://climate.umn.edu/doc/ice_out/ice_out_historical.htm

**Statewide Records**

1. Minnesota Climatology Working Group. "Minnesota Climate Extremes." www.dnr.state.mn.us/climate/summaries_and_publications/extremes.html

2. National Centers for Environmental Information. "State Climate Extremes Committee (SCEC). Minnesota." www.ncdc.noaa.gov/extremes/scec/records

3. Minnesota Climatology Working Group. "Historic Wind Chill Temperatures in Minnesota." January 29, 2014. http://climate.umn.edu/doc/journal/historic_windchills.htm

**Twin Cities Records**

1. National Weather Service. "TWIN CITIES CLIMATOLOGICAL VARIATIONS...TEMPERATURES." Data compiled by the Minnesota Climatology Working Group and accessed via http://files.dnr.state.mn.us/natural_resources/climate/twin_cities/alltimet.html

2. National Weather Service. "TWIN CITIES CLIMATOLOGICAL VARIATIONS...PRECIPITATION EXTREMES." Data compiled by the Minnesota Climatology Working Group and accessed via http://files.dnr.state.mn.us/natural_resources/climate/twin_cities/alltimep.html

3. *Ibid.*

4. *Ibid.*

5. Minnesota Climatology Working Group.

"Historic Wind Chill Temperatures in Minnesota." January 29, 2014. http://climate.umn.edu/doc/journal/historic_windchills.htm

**It Could Be Worse**

1. The National Weather Service, Twin Cities/Chanhassen. "Top Ten Snowfalls Per Month," Accessed via the Minnesota Climatology Working Group at http://files.dnr.state.mn.us/natural_resources/climate/twin_cities/monthsno.html

2. Minnesota Climatology Working Group. "Twin Cities Snowfall Event Count and Seasonal Snowfall Summary Statistics." http://climate.umn.edu/doc/twin_cities/snowmsp.htm

**The Schoolchildren's Blizzard**

1. Ford, Alyssa. *Minnpost.* "125 years ago, deadly 'Children's Blizzard' blasted Minnesota." 1/1/2013. www.minnpost.com/minnesota-history/2013/01/125-years-ago-deadly-children-s-blizzard-blasted-minnesota

**Armistice Day Blizzard**

1. Welter, Ben. *StarTribune.* "Nov. 11, 1940: The Armistice Day Blizzard." 11/11/2014. www.startribune.com/nov-11-1940-the-armistice-day-blizzard/282293811/

**Halloween Blizzard of 1991**

1. National Centers for Environmental Information. "This Month in Climate History: Halloween Blizzard of 1991." www.ncdc.noaa.gov/news/month-climate-history-halloween-blizzard-1991

### The Nation's Icebox?

1. National Centers for Environmental Information. "State Climate Extremes Committee (SCEC). Minnesota." www.ncdc.noaa.gov/extremes/scec/records

2. Mount Washington Observatory. "Normal, Means, and Extremes, 1981-2010." www.mountwashington.org/visit-us/weather-station-tours.aspx

### It Could Be Worse

1. *U.S. National Climatic Data Center.* Data compiled by *USA Today.* "Each State's Low Temperature Record." http://usatoday30.usatoday.com/weather/wcstates.htm

### What's With All the Static?

1. Columbia University, New York City. Go Ask Alice. "Hot and Bothered by Static Electric Shocks." 2/22/2013. http://goaskalice.columbia.edu/hot-and-bothered-static-electric-shocks

2. Alberto-Culver USA. "Static Guard Material Data Safety Sheet." Accessed via: www.msds.com

3. Columbia University, New York City. Go Ask Alice. "Hot and Bothered by Static Electric Shocks." 2/22/2013. http://goaskalice.columbia.edu/hot-and-bothered-static-electric-shocks

### It Could Be Worse

1. Legler, Gretchen. "Science in Antarctica." University of Maine, Farmington. http://faculty.umf.maine.edu/~legler/antarcticawebsite/sci5.htm

### What Was That Thump?!

1. CBS Minnesota. Good Question. "Why Do Our House Make Noise When It's Cold?" 1/7/2014. http://minnesota.cbslocal.com/2014/01/07/good-question-why-do-our-houses-make-noise-when-its-cold

### Preventing Chapped Lips

1. Bennett, Howard. The Washington Post, Kidspost. "Ever Wonder Why Your Lips Get Chapped?" 12/20/2010. www.washingtonpost.com/wp-dyn/content/article/2010/12/19/AR2010121903544.html

2. Gibson, Lawrence. Mayo Clinic. Mayoclinic.org, Diseases and Conditions. "Chapped Lips: What's the Best Remedy?" 05/21/2013. www.mayoclinic.org/diseases-conditions/dry-skin/expert-answers/chapped-lips-faq-20057819

### Feel Gloomy Every Winter? It Could Be Seasonal Affective Disorder

1. Kurlansik SL, Ibay AD. "Seasonal affective disorder. (Review)" Am Fam Physician. Vol. 86, 11 (1037-41). www.aafp.org/afp/2012/1201/p1037.html

### It Could Be Worse

1. Arendt, J. "Biological rhythms during residence in polar regions. (review)" Chronobiol Int. Vol. 29, 4 (379-94). www.ncbi.nlm.nih.gov/pmc/articles/PMC3793275/

### Understanding Weather Warnings and Watches

1. National Oceanographic and Atmospheric Administration. The National Weather Ser-

vice Glossary. "Warning." http://w1.weather.gov/glossary/index.php?letter=w

2. National Oceanographic and Atmospheric Administration. The National Weather Service Glossary. "Watch." http://w1.weather.gov/glossary/index.php?letter=w.

**The Details About Weather Warnings**

1. National Oceanographic and Atmospheric Administration. The National Weather Service Glossary. "Winter Storm Warning." http://w1.weather.gov/glossary/index.php?letter=w.

2. Midwest Regional Climate Center. "Living with Weather: Winter Storms." http://mrcc.isws.illinois.edu/living_wx/winterstorms/index.html

3. *Ibid.*

4. Minnesota Climatology Working Group. "Twin Cities Wind Chill Temperature History." www.dnr.state.mn.us/climate/twin_cities/mspwindchill.html

**Understanding Weather Watches**

1. National Oceanographic and Atmospheric Administration. NOAA News. "NOAA'S NATIONAL WEATHER SERVICE SAYS: KNOW YOUR WINTER WEATHER TERMS." October 2001. www.noaanews.noaa.gov/stories/s794c.htm

2. *Ibid.*

3. National Oceanographic and Atmospheric Administration. "Monitoring and Understanding Our Changing Planet: When Cold Winds Blow." www.noaa.gov/features/monitoring_0209/coldwinds.html

4. National Oceanographic and Atmospheric Administration. The National Weather Service Glossary. "Lake Effect." http://w1.weather.gov/glossary/index.php?letter=l.

**Wind Chill Chart**

1. National Weather Service. Winter Safety: Windchill Chart: www.nws.noaa.gov/om/winter/windchill.shtml

**What Is Wind Chill and Why Does It Matter?**

1. National Weather Service. Winter Safety: Windchill Chart: www.nws.noaa.gov/om/winter/windchill.shtml

2. Big Think. "In Defense of Windchill." http://bigthink.com/the-weather-geek/in-defense-of-wind-chill

3. Collins, Bob. Minnesota Public Radio Blog: Newscut. "Why the wind chill temperature deserves our cold shoulder." January 3, 2014. http://blogs.mprnews.org/newscut/2014/01/why-the-wind-chill-temperature-deserves-our-cold-shoulder/

**Wind Chill Facts**

1. National Weather Service. "Storm Safety: Windchill Questions and Answers." www.nws.noaa.gov/om/winter/windchill.shtmlwww.nws.noaa.gov/om/winter/faqs.shtml

2. Skilling, Tom. *Chicago Tribune.* "Ask Tom: Is Frostbite likely sticking hand out of moving car in 34 degrees?" 1/1/2015. www.chicagotribune.com/news/weather/ct-wea-0122-asktom-20150121-column.html

3. The Mayo Clinic. "Diseases and Conditions; Hypothermia." June 18, 2014. Rochester: Minnesota. www.mayoclinic.org/diseases-conditions/hypothermia/basics/definition/con-20020453

4. Berko J, Ingram DD, Saha S, Parker JD. Deaths attributed to heat, cold, and other weather events in the United States, 2006–2010. National health statistics reports; no 76. Hyattsville, MD: National Center for Health Statistics. 2014. www.cdc.gov/nchs/data/nhsr/nhsr076.pdf

5. Pheifer, Pat. *StarTribune*. "Cold contributed to deaths of 26 in Minnesota." 3/14/2014. www.startribune.com/local/south/250421551.html

### It Could be Worse

1. Accuweather. "Antarctica Weather: South Pole Station." Temperature checked on May 7, 2015. www.accuweather.com/en/antarctica-weather

### Snow

1. Libbrecht, Kenneth. Snowcrystals.com. "Guide to Snowflakes." Pasadena: California Institute of Technology. www.its.caltech.edu/~atomic/snowcrystals/class/class.htm
2. Libbrecht, Kenneth. Snowcrystals.com. "A Snowflake Primer." Pasadena: California Institute of Technology. www.its.caltech.edu/~atomic/snowcrystals/primer/primer.htm

3. *Ibid.*

### Sleet, Freezing Rain and Graupel

1. National Oceanographic and Atmospheric Administration. The National Weather Service Glossary. "Sleet." http://w1.weather.gov/glossary/index.php?letter=s.

2. National Oceanographic and Atmospheric Administration. The National Weather Service Glossary. "Freezing Rain." http://w1.weather.gov/glossary/index.php?letter=f.

3. National Snow and Ice Data Center. "Introduction to Snow." http://nsidc.org/cryosphere/snow/index.html

### Black Ice

1. Minnesota Department of Transportation. "Work Zone Safety: Watch Out for Black Ice." www.dot.state.mn.us/workzone/blackice.html

### Frost

1. Libbrecht, Kenneth. Snowcrystals.com. "Guide to Frost." Pasadena: California Institute of Technology. www.its.caltech.edu/~atomic/snowcrystals/frost/frost.htm

2. National Oceanographic and Atmospheric Administration. The National Weather Service Glossary. "Frost." http://forecast.weather.gov/glossary.php?word=FROST

### Surface Hoar Frost

1. Libbrecht, Kenneth. Snowcrystals.com. "Guide to Frost." Pasadena: California Institute of Technology. www.its.caltech.edu/~atomic/snowcrystals/frost/frost.htm

2. *Ibid.*

### Eskimo Words for Snow

1. Kaplan, Lawrence. 2003. Inuit Snow

Terms: How Many and What Does It Mean? In: Building Capacity in Arctic Societies: Dynamics and shifting perspectives. Proceedings from the 2nd IPSSAS Seminar. Iqaluit, Nunavut, Canada: May 26-June 6, 2003, ed. by François Trudel. Montreal: CIÉRA -- Faculté des sciences sociales Université Laval.

2. Kaplan, Lawrence. Alaska Native Language Center: University of Fairbanks. "Inuit or Eskimo: Which name to use?" www.uaf.edu/anlc/resources/inuit-eskimo/

3. Kaplan, Lawrence. 2003. Inuit Snow Terms: How Many and What Does It Mean? In: Building Capacity in Arctic Societies: Dynamics and shifting perspectives. Proceedings from the 2nd IPSSAS Seminar. Iqaluit, Nunavut, Canada: May 26-June 6, 2003, ed. by François Trudel. Montreal: CIÉRA -- Faculté des sciences sociales Université Laval.

### Wet Snow vs. Dry Snow
1. Libbrecht, Kenneth. Snowcrystals.com. "Is It Really True that No Two Snowflake Crystals are Alike?" Pasadena: California Institute of Technology. www.its.caltech.edu/~atomic/snowcrystals/alike/alike.htm

2. Siegel, Ethan. Science Blogs: *Starts with a Bang.* "Snow Day! Powdery, sticky, icy or slushy?" 12/30/2009. http://scienceblogs.com/startswithabang/2009/12/30/snow-day-powdery-sticky-ice-or/

### How Much Water Is in All That Snow?
1. National Oceanographic and Atmospheric Administration, Eastern Region Headquarters. "Snowfall/Meltwater Table." www.erh.noaa.gov/box/tables/snowfall-meltwater.html

2. *Ibid.*

3. *Ibid.*

### Meltwater Equivalent Chart
1. National Oceanographic and Atmospheric Administration, Eastern Region Headquarters. "Snowfall/Meltwater Table." www.erh.noaa.gov/box/tables/snowfall-meltwater.html

### Sun dogs and Haloes
1. WW2010, Weather World 2010. "Sundogs, mock suns or parhelia." University of Illinois at Urbana-Champaign. http://ww2010.atmos.uiuc.edu/(Gh)/guides/mtr/opt/ice/sd.rxml

2. Nave, Carl R. *Hyperphysics.* "The 22° Halo." Atlanta: Georgia State University, Department of Physics and Astronomy. http://hyperphysics.phy-astr.gsu.edu/hbase/atmos/halo22.html

3. Cowley, Les. Atmospheric Optics. "Tangent Arcs." www.atoptics.co.uk/halo/column.htm

### Sun Pillars
1. Cowley, Les. Atmospheric Optics. "Pillars." www.atoptics.co.uk/halo/column.htmwww.atoptics.co.uk/halo/pillar.htm

### Mirages
1. Young, Andrew T. "A Green Flash Web Page." San Diego: San Diego State University

Astronomy Department. www-rohan.sdsu. edu/~aty/mirages/mirintro.html

2. www.atoptics.co.uk/fz150.htm

**Strange but True: Sir John Ross**

1. In collaboration with Ernest S. Dodge, "ROSS, Sir JOHN," in Dictionary of Canadian Biography, vol. 8, University of Toronto/Université Laval, 2003–www.biographi.ca/en/bio/ross_john_8E.html.

**Rime**

1. Libbrecht, Kenneth. Snowcrystals.com. "Guide to Frost." Pasadena: California Institute of Technology. www.its.caltech.edu/~atomic/snowcrystals/frost/frost.htm

2. American Meteorological Society, cited 2014: "Rime." Glossary of Meteorology. [Available online at http://glossary.ametsoc.org/wiki/Rime]

3. National Oceanographic and Atmospheric Administration. The National Weather Service Glossary. "Rime Ice." http://w1.weather.gov/glossary/index.php?word=rime+ice

**Strange but True**

1. Smith, R.N. British Antarctic Survey Bulletins. Bulletin 30, Article 8. "The Freezing Resistance of Antarctic Fish: An Experimental Study of the Death of Supercooled Fish Resulting from Contact with Ice." October, 1972. www.antarctica.ac.uk/documents/bas_bulletins/bulletin30_08.pdf

**Sastrugi**

1. Cook, Sam. Duluth News Tribune. "Sastru-gi Sighting." January 18, 2005. www.duluth-newstribune.com/outdoors/3657542-sastru-gi-sighting

**Thundersnow**

1. National Oceanographic and Atmospheric Administration. National Severe Storms Laboratory: Severe Weather 101, Lightning FAQ. www.nssl.noaa.gov/education/svrwx101/lightning/faq/

**The Lake Effect**

1. Frazier, Steve. My Fox Twin Cities. "Epic Lake Effect Snows Approach All Time Record." www.myfoxtwincities.com/story/27432272/epic-lake-effect-snows-approach-all-time-record

2. National Oceanographic and Atmospheric Administration, National Weather Service. Buffalo Forecast Office. "Buffalo 2014-15 Winter Summary." www.weather.gov/buf/wintersummary1415

**Lake Superior Freezing Over**

1. National Oceanographic and Atmospheric Administration, Great Lakes Environmental Research Laboratory. "Great Lakes Ice Cover: Annual Maximum Ice Cover, Lake Superior." www.glerl.noaa.gov/data/ice/imgs/sup.jpg

**Ice Tsunamis**

1. CBS Minnesota. "High Winds Create 'Ice Tsunami' on Mille Lacs Lake." May 11, 2013. http://minnesota.cbslocal.com/2013/05/11/high-winds-send-ice-surging-on-to-shore-of-mille-lacs-lake/

### What About the Polar Vortex?

1. National Oceanographic and Atmospheric Administration, Scijinks. "What is a Polar Vortex?" http://scijinks.jpl.nasa.gov/polar-vortex/

2. *Ibid.*

### Assemble a Winter Emergency Kit

1. Kain, Stan. National Oceanographic and Atmospheric Administration, Eastern Regional Headquarters. "Safe Winter Travel." www.srh.noaa.gov/oun/?n=safety-winter-safetykit

### Tune Up Your Furnace or Heating Element

1. Xu, Jiaquan. "Average Annual Number of Deaths and Death Rates from Unintentional, Non-Fire Related Carbon Monoxide Poisoning, by Sex and Age Group, United States, 1999-2010." MMWR 2014;63:[65]. www.cdc.gov/mmwr/preview/mmwrhtml/mm6303a6.htm

2. Minnesota Department of Health. MNPH Data Access. "CO Poisoning Deaths: Facts & Figures (by year)" https://apps.health.state.mn.us/mndata/carbon_monoxide_deaths#deaths_line

3. Minnesota Department of Public Safety. "Winter Hazard Awareness and Safety Information, Winter Safety Checklist, Home Preparedness." https://dps.mn.gov/divisions/hsem/weather-awareness-preparedness/Documents/Winter Safety Checklist - HOME.pdf

4. *Ibid.*

5. Mr. Heater.com, Frequently Asked Questions. "WHY CAN THE BUDDY HEATERS BE USED INDOORS SAFELY?" 6/25/2014. www.mrheater.com/faqs/general/Why-can-the-Buddy-heaters-be-used-indoors-safely/

6. U.S. Department of Energy, Energy.gov. "Portable Heaters." 12/15/2014. http://energy.gov/energysaver/articles/portable-heaters

7. Mr. Heater.com, Frequently Asked Questions. "WHY CAN THE BUDDY HEATERS BE USED INDOORS SAFELY?" 6/25/2014. www.mrheater.com/faqs/general/Why-can-the-Buddy-heaters-be-used-indoors-safely/

### Winter Fire Safety

1. Minnesota Department of Public Safety. "Winter Fire Safety Fact Sheet." https://dps.mn.gov/divisions/sfm/public-education/Documents/Fact sheets/Winter-fire-safety-fact-sheet.pdf

### Caulking Gaps in Windows and Doors

1. U.S. Department of Energy, Energy.gov. "Savings Project: How to Seal Air Leaks with Caulk." http://energy.gov/energysaver/projects/savings-project-how-seal-air-leaks-caulk

### High-efficiency Windows/Doors and Upgrading Insulation

1. U.S. Department of Energy, Energy.gov. "Energy-Efficient Windows." 2/18/2015. http://energy.gov/energysaver/articles/energy-efficient-windows

2. U.S. Department of Energy, Energy.gov. "Energy Performance Ratings for Windows, Doors, and Skylights." 1/21/2015. http://energy.gov/energysaver/articles/energy-performance-ratings-windows-doors-and-skylights

**Preventing Frozen Pipes**

1. Trattner, Douglas. House Logic. "How to Prevent Freezing Pipes." www.houselogic. com/home-advice/plumbing/prevent-freezing-pipes/

2. *Ibid.*

**Unfreezing a Pipe**

1. American Red Cross. "Winter Storm Preparedness: Preventing and Thawing Frozen Pipes." www.redcross.org/prepare/disaster/winter-storm/preventing-thawing-frozen-pipes

2. *Ibid.*

**Upgrading Insulation**

1. U.S. Department of Energy, Energy Efficiency and Renewable Energy. "R-Value Recommendations for Buildings." http://web.ornl.gov/cgi-bin/cgiwrap?user=roofs&script=ZipTable/ins_fact.pl

2. U.S. Department of Energy, Energy.gov. "Adding Insulation to an Existing Home." April 27, 2015. http://energy.gov/energysaver/articles/adding-insulation-existing-home

**Find Other Drafts**

1. U.S. Department of Energy. http://energy.gov/

2. U.S. Department of Energy, Environmental Energy Technologies Division, Lawrence Berkeley National Laboratory. "Home Energy Saver." http://hes.lbl.gov/consumer/.

**Get Help from the Pros**

U.S. Department of Energy. "Energy Saver, Home Weatherization, Home Energy Audits." http://energy.gov/public-services/homes/home-weatherization/home-energy-audits

**Winterizing Outside the House**

1. Fay, Karie. Realestate.com. "A Checklist for Winterizing and Weatherproofing Your Home." 11/18/2012. www.realestate.com/advice/a-checklist-for-winterizing-and-weatherproofing-your-home-66175/

2. Apartment Therapy. "Do It Now: Be Sure to Shut Off Your Hose Bibs for the Winter." www.apartmenttherapy.com/why-its-so-important-to-shut-off-your-hose-bibs-for-the-winter-198050

3. Minnesota Department of Public Safety. "Winter Hazard Awareness and Safety Information, Winter Safety Checklist, Home Preparedness." https://dps.mn.gov/divisions/hsem/weather-awareness-preparedness/Documents/Winter Safety Checklist - HOME.pdf

**How to Layer**

1. Tischler, Steve. REI.com. "Learn at REI, Expert Advice, Layering Basics." 1/22/2015. www.rei.com/learn/expert-advice/layering-basics.html

**It Could Be Worse**

1. Cherry-Garrard, Apsley. *The Worst Journey in the World, Volumes 1 and 2.* 1921. www.gutenberg.org/ebooks/14363

**Base Layer**

1. Moss, Tim. The Next Challenge.com "Comparison of Base Layer Materials." 9/2/2014. http://thenextchallenge.org/

comparison-base-layer-materials/#synthetic-base-layers

2. Cramer, Jack. Outdoorgearlab.com. "Side-by-Side Comparison - Long Underwear." 3/30/2015. www.outdoorgearlab.com/Long-Underwear-Reviews/compare?

### Insulating Layer

1. Tischler, Steve. REI.com. "Learn at REI, Expert Advice, Layering Basics." 1/22/2015. www.rei.com/learn/expert-advice/layering-basics.html

### Explaining Jacket Fill Amounts

1. Simrell, Chris and McKenzie Long. "How to Choose the Best Down Jacket." 11/26/2014. www.outdoorgearlab.com/Down-Jacket-Reviews/Buying-Advice#Down-Fill-Powers

### What is Down, Exactly, and Where Does it Come From?

1. Canada-Goose.com. "Our Materials, A Word About Down." www.canada-goose.com/our-materials/our-story-canada-goose-about-our-product-our-materials.html

### Strange but True

1. Merriam-Webster.com. "Balaclava." 2011. www.merriam-webster.com/dictionary/balaclava

### Shoes, Boots and Socks

1. Kuklane, Kalev. "Protection of Feet in Cold Exposure." *Industrial Health*. 37, 2009. (242-253). Accessed via: www.jstage.jst.go.jp/article/indhealth/47/3/47_3_242/_pdf

### Dressing for Winter Exercise

1. Mayo Clinic Staff. "Winter fitness: Safety tips for exercising outdoors." Fitness. 02/05/2014. www.mayoclinic.org/healthy-lifestyle/fitness/in-depth/fitness/art-20045626

### Keep Your Kids in Mind and Don't Forget Your Furry Friends

1. American Society for Prevention of Cruelty to Animals. ASPCA.org. "Pet Care, Top Ten Winter Skin & Paw Care Tips." www.aspca.org/pet-care/top-ten-winter-skin-paw-care-tips

### Frostbite

1. Bensouilah, Janetta and Philippa Buck. Aromadermatology: *Aromatherapy in the Treatment and Care of Common Skin Conditions*. Radcliffe Publishing, 2006. Chapter 1, "Skin Structure and Formation." Accessed from Course Materials of Bioengineering 237, Bioengineering Solids and Fluids Lab. Professor Chris Niels at the University of Washington. Accessed via: http://courses.washington.edu/bioen327/Labs/Lit_SkinStruct_Bensouilah_Ch01.pdf

2. *Ibid*.

3. Mayo Clinic Staff. "Frostbite." Stages of Frostbite. 10/15/2014. www.mayoclinic.org/diseases-conditions/frostbite/multimedia/stages-frostbite/flh-20078312

### Frostnip

1. Mayo Clinic Staff. "Frostbite." Frostbite Symptoms. 10/15/2014. www.mayoclinic. org/diseases-conditions/frostbite/basics/ symptoms/con-20034608

2. *Ibid.*

### Superficial Frostbite

1. Mayo Clinic Staff. "Frostbite." Frostbite Symptoms. 10/15/2014. www.mayoclinic. org/diseases-conditions/frostbite/basics/ symptoms/con-20034608

2. University of Maryland Medical Center. "Frostbite." 7/9/2015. http://umm.edu/ health/medical/altmed/condition/frostbite

### Severe/Deep Frostbite

1. Mechen, C. Crawford and Dirk M. Elston (ed.) Medscape. "Frostbite." 11/4/2014. http://emedicine.medscape.com/article/926249-overview#a0104

2. Google search if you dare: https://images. google.com "frostbite"

### It Could Be Worse

1. Cartographia. "Hannibal Crosses the Alps." 6/2/2008. https://cartographia. wordpress.com/2008/06/02/hannibal-crosses-the-alps/

2. Lexikon der Wehrmacht. "Medal for the Winter battle in the East, 1941-1942, known as the 'East Medal (my translation).'" www. lexikon-der-wehrmacht.de/Orden/mwio.html

### How Long Does It Take to Get Frostbite?

1. Mayo Clinic Staff. "Frostbite." Frostbite Symptoms. 10/15/2014. www.mayoclinic. org/diseases-conditions/frostbite/basics/ symptoms/con-20034608

### Frostbite Treatment

1. Centers for Disease Control and Prevention. "Frostbite." Emergency Preparedness and Response. www.bt.cdc.gov/disasters/ winter/staysafe/frostbite.asp

2. *Ibid.*

### How Not to Treat Frostbite

1. Centers for Disease Control and Prevention. "Frostbite." Emergency Preparedness and Response. www.bt.cdc.gov/disasters/ winter/staysafe/frostbite.asp

### How to Avoid Frostbite

1. Antti-Poika I., Pohjolainen T. Alaranta H. "Severe frostbite of the upper extremities—a psychosical problem mostly associated with alcohol abuse." *Scand J. Soc. Med*, 1990; 18:59-61. http://sjp.sagepub.com/content/18/4/273.extract

### The Science of Frostbite

1. Dana AS, Jr., Rex IH, Jr., Samitz MH. "The Hunting Reaction." *Arch Dermatol.* 1969; 99(4):441-450 .http://archderm.jamanetwork.com/article.aspx?articleid=530922

2. U.S. National Library of Medicine. Medline Plus. "Frostbite." 1/13/2014. www.nlm.nih. gov/medlineplus/ency/article/000057.htm

3. Hogan, David and Jonathan Burstein. *Disaster* Medicine. Lippincott Williams & Wilkins, 2007. Accessed via books.google.com

### Hypothermia

1. Minnesota Sea Grant. "Hypothermia Prevention: Survival in Cold Water." 10/15/2014. www.seagrant.umn.edu/coastal_communities/hypothermia#what

2. Centers for Disease Control and Prevention. "Hypothermia." Emergency Preparedness and Response. 12/3/2012. http://emergency.cdc.gov/disasters/winter/staysafe/hypothermia.asp

3. *Ibid.*

4. Danzl, Daniel. *Merck Manual, Consumer Edition.* "Hypothermia." www.merckmanuals.com/home/injuries-and-poisoning/cold-injuries/hypothermia

5. Minnesota Department of Natural Resources. "Minnesota Ice-Related Fatalities, 1976-2014." http://files.dnr.state.mn.us/education_safety/safety/ice/ice_stats.pdf

6. *Ibid.*

### Hypothermia Symptoms

1. Mayo Clinic Staff. "Hypothermia." Hypothermia Symptoms. 6/18/2014. www.mayoclinic.org/diseases-conditions/hypothermia/basics/symptoms/con-20020453

2. *Ibid.*

3. Clinical Key. Elsevier Publishing. "Hypothermia." Emergency Medicine. www.clinicalkey.com/topics/emergency-medicine/hypothermia.html

4. U.S. National Library of Medicine. Medline Plus. "Hypovolemic shock." 1/13/2014. www.nlm.nih.gov/medlineplus/ency/article/000167.htm

5. Centers for Disease Control and Prevention. "Hypothermia." Emergency Preparedness and Response. 12/3/2012. http://emergency.cdc.gov/disasters/winter/staysafe/hypothermia.asp

### Hypothermia Treatment

1. Centers for Disease Control and Prevention. "Hypothermia." Emergency Preparedness and Response. 12/3/2012. http://emergency.cdc.gov/disasters/winter/staysafe/hypothermia.asp

2. *Ibid.*

3. Mayo Clinic Staff. "Hypothermia: First Aid." 3/31/2015. www.mayoclinic.org/first-aid/first-aid-hypothermia/basics/art-20056624

### Brought Back from the Brink

1. Hilmo, Jonas *et al.* "'Nobody is dead until warm and dead': Prolonged resuscitation is warranted in arrested hypothermic victims also in remote areas – A retrospective study from northern Norway"

Resuscitation 85, 9 (1204-1211) www.sciencedirect.com/science/article/pii/S0300957214005243

2. Schmidt U, Fritz KW, Kasperczyk W, Tscherne H. "Successful resuscitation of a child with severe hypothermia after cardiac arrest of 88 minutes." *Prehosp Disaster Med.* 10, 1 (60-62).www.ncbi.nlm.nih.gov/pubmed/10155409

3. Lexow K. "Severe accidental hypothermia: survival after 6 hours 30 minutes of cardio-pulmonary resuscitation." *Arctic Med Res.* 50 Suppl, 6 (112-114). www.ncbi.nlm.nih.gov/pubmed/1811563

### Strange but True

1. Tveita T. "Rewarming from hypothermia. Newer aspects on the pathophysiology of re-warming shock (Review)." Int. J Circumpolar Health, 59, 3-4. (260-266.) www.ncbi.nlm.nih.gov/pubmed/11209678

2. McCullough L, Arora S. "Diagnosis and treatment of hypothermia (Review)." *Am Fam Physician.* Vol. 70, 12 (2325-2332). www.aafp.org/afp/2004/1215/p2325.html

### The Diving Reflex

1. Minnesota Sea Grant. "What is the mammalian diving reflex?" 10/15/2014. www.seagrant.umn.edu/coastal_communities/hypothermia#mammalian

2. Nielsen, Niklas, Jørn Wetterslev, Tobias Cronberg, David Erlinge, Yvan Gasche, Christian Hassager, Janneke Horn, *et al.* Targeted temperature management at 33°C versus 36°C after cardiac arrest. *New England Journal of Medicine* 369, 23 (2197-206), http://archive-ouverte.unige.ch/unige:35178 (accessed July 9, 2015).

3. Wise MP, Horn J, Åneman A, Nielsen N. "Targeted temperature management after out-of-hospital cardiac arrest: certainties and uncertainties." *Crit Care.* Vol. 18, 4. (459). http://ccforum.com/content/18/4/459

### Paradoxical Undressing

1. Wedin B, Vanggaard L, Hirvonen J. "Paradoxical undressing." in fatal hypothermia. J Forensic Sci. Vol. 24, 3, (543-553). www.ncbi.nlm.nih.gov/pubmed/541627

### Terminal Burrowing

1. Rothschild MA, Schneider V. "Terminal burrowing behaviour–a phenomenon of lethal hypothermia." Int J Legal Med. Vol. 107, 5. (250-6). http://link.springer.com/article/10.1007%2FBF01245483

### Trench Foot

1. Danzl, Daniel. *Merck Manual, Professional Edition.* "Nonfreezing Tissue Injuries." www.merckmanuals.com/home/injuries-and-poisoning/cold-injuries/hypothermia

2. *Ibid.*

3. Atenstaedt RL. "Trench foot: the medical response in the first World War 1914-18." *Wilderness Environ Med.* Vol. 17, 4 (282-289). www.ncbi.nlm.nih.gov/pubmed/17219792

### Chillblains

1. Mayo Clinic Staff. "Chillblains." Diseases and Conditions. 12/06/2006. www.mayoclinic.org/diseases-conditions/chilblains/basics/causes/con-20033727

2. Vano-Galvan, Sergio, and Antonio Martorell. "Chilblains." CMAJ : Canadian Medical Association Journal Vol., 184, 1 (67)

### Sunburn in the Winter

1. Mayo Clinic Staff. "Do you need sunscreen in the winter?" Health Tip. 1/15/2013. www.mayoclinic.org/health-tip/art-20048629

### Shoveling Tips

1. Janardhanan R, Henry Z, et al. "The snow-shoveler's ST elevation myocardial infarction." *Am J Cardiol*. Vol 106, 4 (596-600). www.ncbi.nlm.nih.gov/pubmed/20691323

### Snowblower Selection

1. Snowblower.com. "Explaining the Design of Snowblowers." 10/01/2010. www.snowblower.com/articles/explaining-the-design-of-snowblowers-1319.html

### Snowblower Safety

1. Jardin E, et al. "Snowblower injuries to the hand. (Review)" *Chir Main*. Vol. 33, 4 (272-8). www.ncbi.nlm.nih.gov/pubmed/24996696

2. Hammig B, Jones C. "Injuries related to snow blowers in the United States: 2002 through 2008." *Acad Emerg Med*. Vol. 17, 5 (566-9). http://onlinelibrary.wiley.com/doi/10.1111/j.1553-2712.2010.00730.x/full

### Note About Rock Salt

1. Hart, Lindsey. Blandon Family Veterinarian. "The Dangers of Rock Salt For Your Pet." 11/29/2012. www.blandonfamilyvet.com/2012/11/29/the-dangers-of-rock-salt-for-your-pet/

### Signs of an Ice Dam

1. Travelers Insurance. "Tips to Remove Ice Dams." Weather Safety, Winter Storms. www.travelers.com/prepare-prevent/mother-nature/winter-storm-safety/ice-dam-removal.aspx

### Removing an Ice Dam

1. Hurst-Wajszczuk, Joe. "Fast Fixes for Ice Dams." House Exterior, Roofing www.thisoldhouse.com/toh/article/0,,1131314,00.html

2. *Ibid*.

3. Home Partners. "Ice Dams – Several quick fixes but only one cure." http://home-partners.com/articles/ice-dams-quick-fixes-cure

### It Could Be Worse

1. Nave, Carl R. *Hyperphysics*. "Impact Force from Falling Object." Atlanta: Georgia State University, Department of Physics and Astronomy. http://hyperphysics.phy-astr.gsu.edu/hbase/flobi.html#c1

2. Atha, et al. "The damaging punch." *British Medical Journal*, Vol. 29, 1 (21-28). http://europepmc.org/backend/ptpmcrender.fcgi?accid=PMC1419171&blobtype=pdf

### How Much Snow is Too Much for the Roof to Handle?

1. Berendsohn, Roy. *Popular Mechanics*. "How Much Snow is Too Much for Your Roof?" 2/17/2012. www.popularmechanics.com/home/outdoor-projects/how-to/a7333/how-much-snow-is-too-much-for-your-roof/

2. Eakes, Jon. "Ask Jon Eakes: When do I need to remove snow from a roof?" 3/11/2008. http://joneakes.com/jons-fixit-da-

tabase/2085-OVERVIEW-When-do-I-need-to-remove-snow-from-a-roof

**Shoveling the Deck**
1. Wormer, Andrew. Professional Deck Builder. "With More Snow in the Forecast, Are Decks at Risk?" Engineering. 2/13/2015. www.deckmagazine.com/engineering/with-more-snow-in-the-forecast-are-decks-at-risk_o.aspx

**How to Walk in Winter: Embrace Your Inner Penguin**
1. Mayo Clinic Health System. "Don't let icy sidewalks get you down." Hometown Health Blog. 12/07/2013. http://mayoclinichealthsystem.org/hometown-health/speaking-of-health/dont-let-icy-sidewalks-get-you-down

2. Bourassa, Sarah. Today. "Stay safe on the ice by walking like this animal." www.today.com/health/stay-safe-ice-walk-penguin-2D12108872

**Sad but True**
1. Centers for Disease Control and Prevention, National Center for Health Statistics. Underlying Cause of Death 1999-2013 on CDC WONDER Online Database, released 2015. Data are from the Multiple Cause of Death Files, 1999-2013, as compiled from data provided by the 57 vital statistics jurisdictions through the Vital Statistics Cooperative Program. Accessed at http://wonder.cdc.gov/ucd-icd10.html

**Your Car's Battery**
1. Consumer Reports. "Q&A: Why do car batteries die in winter?" Consumer Reports News. 11/27/2009. www.consumerreports.org/cro/news/2009/11/q-a-why-do-car-batteries-die-in-winter/index.htm

2. American Automobile Association. "Winter Car Care Tips." www.aaa.com/aaa/047/PDF/WinterTips.pdf

3. Interstate Batteries. "Winter Car Battery Checklist." http://corporate.interstatebatteries.com/winterizing_batteries/

**Stay Up To Date With Your Maintenance**
1. Consumer Reports. "How to winterize a car." Consumer Reports News. 10/2013. www.consumerreports.org/cro/2012/12/winterizing-your-vehicle/index.htm

2. Noria Corporation. "Cold Weather and Oil Changes: What You Need to Know." www.machinerylubrication.com/Read/1800/cold-wear-oil-changes-what-you-need-to-know

**Windshield Wipers**
1. Ford Motor Company. "Our Products." www.fordparts.com/Commerce/

2. Ken's Car Tips. "All Washer Fluids Are Not Created Equal." 12/6/2013. http://kenscartips.com/2013/12/06/all-washer-fluids-are-not-created-equal/

**Defroster and Heat**
1. Blake's Auto Body. "Car Heater Malfunctions and Maintenance." http://blakesautobody.com/driving-tips-and-facts/car-heater-malfunctions-and-maintenance/

**Gas It Up**

1. Gold Eagle. "HEET Brand FAQ's." www.goldeagle.com/brands/heet-faqs

**Assemble Your Car Kit**

1. Kain, Stan. National Oceanographic and Atmopsheric Administration, Eastern Regional Headquarters. "Safe Winter Travel." www.srh.noaa.gov/oun/?n=safety-winter-safetykit

**Start Your Car and Let it Warm Up (But Not For Too Long)**

1. Mooney, Chris. *The Washington Post.* "The biggest winter energy myth: That you need to idle your car before driving." 12/29/2014. www.washingtonpost.com/blogs/wonkblog/wp/2014/12/29/the-biggest-winter-energy-myth-that-you-need-to-idle-your-car-before-driving/

2. Torchinsky, Jason. Jalopnik. "Yes, Warm Your Damn Car Up If It's Cold." 1/08/2015. http://jalopnik.com/yes-warm-your-damn-car-up-if-its-cold-1678251730

**Bundle Up and Hit the Road**

1. Minnesota Department of Public Safety. "WINTER SAFETY CHECKLIST - FOR DRIVING AND TRAVEL." https://dps.mn.gov/divisions/hsem/weather-awareness-preparedness/Documents/Winter%20Safety%20Checklist%20-%20TRAVEL.pdf

**Whose Responsibility Is It to Plow?**

1. Williams, John. Minnesota House Research, Short Subjects. "Minnesota Highway Mileage." 09/2005. www.house.leg.state.mn.us/hrd/pubs/ss/ssmnhm.pdf

**Plow Safety**

1. Minnesota Department of Transportation. "Snowplow facts." Workzone Safety. www.dot.state.mn.us/workzone/snow-plow-facts.html

2. Minnesota Department of Public Safety. "Winter Car Safety, Snowplow Safety." https://dps.mn.gov/divisions/hsem/weather-awareness-preparedness/Documents/Snowplow Safety.pdf

**Road Salt and Why It Works**

1. Minnesota Local Road Research Board. Minnesota Snow and Ice Control, Field Handbook for Snowplow Operators, Second Revision. www.mnltap.umn.edu/publications/handbooks/documents/snowice.pdf

2. U.S. Geological Survey. "Salt." Mineral Commodity Summaries. 02/2014. http://minerals.usgs.gov/minerals/pubs/commodity/salt/mcs-2014-salt.pdf

**Where Does It Come From?**

1. U.S. Geological Survey. "Salt." Mineral Commodity Summaries. 02/2014. http://minerals.usgs.gov/minerals/pubs/commodity/salt/mcs-2014-salt.pdf

2. Detroit Salt Company. "History of The Detroit Salt Mine." http://detroitsalt.com/history/

**Road Salt and Water Quality**

1. Minnesota Pollution Control Agency. Metropolitan Area Chloride Project. "Road salt and water quality." www.pca.state.mn.us/index.php/water/water-types-and-programs/

minnesotas-impaired-waters-and-tmdls/tm-dl-projects/special-projects/metro-area-chloride-project/road-salt-and-water-quality.html

2. Murphy, Dan and Heinz Stefan. University of Minnesota "Project Report No. 485: Seasonal Salinity Cycles in Eight Lakes of the Minneapolis/St. Paul Metropolitan Area." St. Anthony Falls Laboratory, Engineering, Environmental and Geophysical Fluid Dynamics. October 2006. https://conservancy.umn.edu/bitstream/handle/11299/113692/pr485.pdf?sequence=1

**So You Got Stuck In Your Driveway**
1. Bryant, Jefferson. Knowhow.napaonline.com "NAPA KNOW-HOW NOTES: 10 TIPS ON HOW TO GET YOUR CAR UNSTUCK." 2/2/15. http://knowhow.napaonline.com/napa-know-notes-10-tips-get-car-unstuck/

**It Could Be Worse**
1. Minnesota Department of Public Safety. *Crash Facts.* "2013 Crash Facts." https://dps.mn.gov/divisions/ots/reports-statistics/Documents/2013-crash-facts.pdf

**So Your Door Locks (or Your Entire Handle) Are Frozen**
1. Girls Auto Clinic. "'I CAN'T GET INTO MY CAR' – CAR DOOR FROZEN SHUT." http://girlsautoclinic.com/car-door-frozen-shut/

2. *Ibid.*

**So Your Car Battery Died**
1. State Farm Insurance. "How to Jump-Start a Car Safely." 12/30/2013. http://learning-center.statefarm.com/auto/safety/how-to-jump-start-a-car-safely/

2. *Ibid.*

3. *Ibid*

**Snow Sculptures**
1. Mohrman, Cristel. Allstate.com. "How to Make a Snow Sculpture." The Allstate Blog. 1/1/2014. http://blog.allstate.com/how-to-make-a-snow-sculpture/

**Snow Forts and Snowball Fights**
1. Niiranen, M, and I Raivio. "Eye Injuries in Children." *The British Journal of Ophthalmology.* Vol. 65, 6 (436–438). www.ncbi.nlm.nih.gov/pmc/articles/PMC1039540/pdf/brjopthal00186-0072.pdf

**Still Don't Believe Me? Here's the Math**
1. My Fox Twin Cities. "Snow Forts: Beware Cave-ins as Temperatures Rise." 02/13/2014. www.myfoxtwincities.com/story/24721357/snow-forts-beware-cave-ins-as-temperatures-rise

2. CBC News, Montreal. "Quebec Man Dies in Snow Fort Collapse." 03/07/2011. www.cbc.ca/news/canada/montreal/que-man-dies-in-snow-fort-collapse-1.1085791

3. Hellevang, Ken. North Dakota State University, Winter Storm Information. "Your Roof Should Be Built To Handle Normal Snow Load." www.ag.ndsu.edu/winterstorm/winter-storm-information-home-1/your-roof-should-be-built-to-handle-normal-snow-load

**Cross-Country Skiing and Snowshoeing**
1. Backcountry.com. "Cross Country Ski Guide." www.backcountry.com/sc/cross-country-ski-guide

**Snowmobiling**

1. Keillor, Lynn. StarTribune. "Snowmobiling 101: How to Rent and Ride in Minnesota." 12/04/2014. www.startribune.com/snowmobiling-101-how-to-rent-and-ride-in-minnesota/284804211/

**The Canadian Pacific Holiday Train**

1. Canadian Pacific Railway. "The CP Holiday Train." www.cpr.ca/holiday-train/canada

**Hanukkah**

1. Chabad.org. "What is Hanukkah?" www.chabad.org/holidays/chanukah/article_cdo/aid/102911/jewish/What-Is-Hanukkah.htm

2. Time and Date AS. "Chanukah/Hanukkah (first day) in United States." Accessed via www.timeanddate.com/holidays/us/chanukah

**Kwanzaa**

1. The Official Kwanzaa Website. "Kwanzaa FAQ." www.officialkwanzaawebsite.org/index.shtml

**The Lunar New Year**

1. Time and Date AS. "Chinese New Year in United States." Accessed via www.timeanddate.com/holidays/us/chinese-new-year

**St. Paul Winter Carnival**

1. St. Paul Winter Carnival. "St. Paul Winter Carnival FAQS." www.wintercarnival.com

**John Beargrease Sled Dog Marathon**

1. John Beargrease Sled Dog Marathon. "About John Beargrease." www.beargrease.com/aboutjohnbeargrease.htm

**The Famous Boiling Water Trick**

1. Wolchover, Natalie. Live Science.

"How Can Boiling Water Turn to Snow?" 01/24/2011. www.livescience.com/32951-how-can-boiling-water-turn-snow.html

**Grow your Own Snow**

1. Libbrecht, Kenneth. Snowcrystals.com. "Grow Your Own Snow Crystals." Pasadena: California Institute of Technology. www.its.caltech.edu/~atomic/snowcrystals/project/project.htm

**Designer Snowflakes**

1. Libbrecht, Kenneth. Snowcrystals.com. "Designer Snowflakes - Part One." Pasadena: California Institute of Technology. www.its.caltech.edu/~atomic/snowcrystals/designer1/designer1.htm

**Freeze a Bubble**

1. Karo Syrup. "Giant Bubbles." Recipes. http://karosyrup.com/Recipe/Giant_Bubbles

**Collect Snowflakes**

1. Libbrecht, Kenneth. Snowcrystals.com. "Preserving Snow Crystals." Pasadena: California Institute of Technology. www.its.caltech.edu/~atomic/snowcrystals/preserve/preserve.htm

**Movies with Minnesota Connections**

1. The Internet Movie Database. www.imbd.com

**Buffalo Wings**

1. Trillin, Calvin. The New Yorker. "An Attempt to Compile a Short History of the Buffalo Chicken Wing." 08/25/1980. www.newyorker.com/magazine/1980/08/25/an-attempt-to-compile-a-short-history-of-the-buffalo-chicken-wing?currentPage=all

2. Anchor Bar, Buffalo. Community Table. "Anchor Bar's Buffalo Wings: The Original Hot Wing Recipe." 01/27/2012. http://communitytable.parade.com/26655/anchorbar-buffalony/anchor-bars-buffalo-wings-the-original-hot-wing-recipe/

**Pho**

1. Ngo, Nancy. *Twin Cities Pioneer Press.* "Pho: where to find big bowls of the best stuff." 01/29/2014. www.twincities.com/restaurants/ci_25019504/pho-where-find-big-bowls-best-stuff

2. Allrecipes.com. "Authentic Pho." http://allrecipes.com/recipe/authentic-pho/

**Lebkuchen, Lefse and other Treats**

1. CBS Minnesota. "Delivery Rooms Brace for Polar Vortex Baby Boom." 09/06/2014. http://minnesota.cbslocal.com/2014/09/06/delivery-rooms-brace-for-polar-vortex-baby-boom/

**Homemade Ice Cream Made Outdoors**

1. Special Fork Blog. "Baby It's Cold Outside: Time for Ice Cream." 11/23/2010. http://specialforkblog.com/2010/11/23/baby-it%E2%80%99s-cold-outside%E2%80%A6time-for-ice-cream/

2. Bartlett, Christina. Del Casa. "How to Make Ice Cream Northern Style (outside in -30)." http://christinabartlett.com/delacasa/2012/12/15/how-to-make-icecream-northern-style-outside-in-30/

**Peppermint Patty**

1. Graham, Colleen. About.com, About Food, Cocktails, Liqueur, Beer and Wine Recipe Collection. "Hot Peppermint Patty." http://cocktails.about.com/od/cocktailrecipes/r/hot_pprmnt_pty.htm

**It Could Be Worse**

1. Halsey, Lewis G. and Mike A. Stroud. "100 Years Since Scott Reached the Pole: A Century of Learning About the Physiological Demands of Antarctica." Physiological Reviews. Vol. 92, 2 (521-536). http://physrev.physiology.org/content/92/2/521.long#F8

**It's Not Just a Nickname**

1. All About Birds. "Arctic Tern." The Cornell Laboratory of Ornithology, Cornell University. www.allaboutbirds.org/guide/Arctic_Tern/id

# Recommended Reading and Websites

National Weather Service, Twin Cities Office
www.weather.gov/mpx/

National Oceanographic and
Atmospheric Administration
www.noaa.gov

Minnesota Climatology Working Group
http://climate.umn.edu
www.dnr.state.mn.us/climate/
twin_cities/index.html

The National Weather Service Glossary
http://w1.weather.gov/glossary/

Minnesota Department of Public Safety
https://dps.mn.gov

National Centers for
Environmental Information
www.ncei.noaa.gov

Great Lakes Environmental
Research Laboratory
www.glerl.noaa.gov

Snowcrystals.com
www.its.caltech.edu/%7Eatomic/
snowcrystals/

The Mayo Clinic
www.mayoclinic.org

The Centers for Disease Control
and Prevention
www.cdc.gov

Atmospheric Optics
www.atoptics.co.uk/halo/column.htm

U.S. Department of Energy
energy.gov

Build a Cloud Chamber
www.lns.cornell.edu/~adf4/
cloud.html

## Photo Credits

Back Cover (left): Brett Ortler. Other cover images via Shutterstock.

12, Brett Ortler 16, (bottom) Brett Ortler 24, Brett Ortler 26, Adapted from National Oceanographic and Atmospheric Administration (noaa.gov) 31, Kenneth Libbrecht (both) 35, (top) adapted from National Oceanographic and Atmospheric Administration (noaa.gov) 35, (bottom) Brett Ortler 36, Brett Ortler 38 (top), Brett Ortler 40, (top) Brett Ortler 42, (top) Maps by NOAA Climate.gov based on NCEP Reanalysis data from NOAA ESRL Physical Sciences Division 42 (bottom), NASA 55, Library of Congress 72, Library of Congress 113, Brett Ortler 123, Brett Ortler 135, Courtesy of Kenneth Libbrecht 168, Kayli Schaaf

The (unaltered) images on the following pages are licensed according to the Creative Commons Attribution 2.0 License, which is accessible here: http://creativecommons.org/licenses/by-sa/2.0/us/

11, "Groundhog Day Stage," Flickr User Pointshoot, available at www.flickr.com/photos/pointshoot/861062345

30, (second from top) "Sleet on the Ground," Flickr User Mike Epp, available at https://simple.wikipedia.org/wiki/Sleet#/media/File:Sleet_on_the_ground.jpg

37, "A Highway Mirage," Flickr User Michael Gil, available at www.flickr.com/photos/msvg/5994891327

106, "Snow," Flickr User Connie, available at www.flickr.com/photos/conbon/3532025263/in/photolist-6o7y4i-q62gV5-8n63nS-nQZXg8-7PT7oR-9RBgdd

107, "Big City Bicycle," Flickr User Dustin Gaffke, available at www.flickr.com/photos/onepointfour/12396753253

110, "Skybridges skyway," Flickr User Thunderchild7 available at www.flickr.com/photos/thunderchild5/536517892/

The (unaltered) images on the following pages are licensed according to the Creative Commons Attribution 2.0 License, which is accessible here: https://creativecommons.org/licenses/by-nd/2.0/

121 (top), "Photo 7," Flickr User Wisconsin Department of Natural Resources, www.flickr.com/photos/widnr/15883034413; note: the author is aware the photo is of WI, not MN, but the photo gives you an idea of what to expect

Many images in this book were sourced from Shutterstock (www.shutterstock.com). All images in this book are being used legally. For information about specific image provenance, please contact the author (www.brettortler.com).

# About the Author

Brett Ortler is an editor at Adventure Publications. He is the author of *Minnesota Trivia Don'tcha Know!*, *The Fireflies Book* and *The Mosquito Book*. His essays, poems and other work appear widely, including in *Salon*, *The Good Men Project*, *The Nervous Breakdown*, *Living Ready* and in a number of other venues in print and online. He lives in the Twin Cities with his wife and their young children.